growing up

Dr. Chuck Ribley's
INNER WINNERS' SEMINARS
20960 TELEGRAPH RD., ROMULUS, MI 48174
(313) 479-2971

I would rather have all the risks which come from free discussion of sex than the greater risks we run by a conspiracy of silence.

> Dr Cosmo Lang
> Archbishop of Canterbury 1928–1942

We have no doubt that children's questions about sex ought to be answered plainly and truthfully whenever they are asked.... (and) if they are able to do it, the proper people to answer these questions are the parents.

> Children & Their Primary Schools
> Central Advisory Council for Education
> (The Plowden Report 1967)

cover shows a group of statues from the
anent exhibition in the Hall of Human Biology
e Natural History Museum, Kensington, London.
aphed by kind permission of The Trustees of The British Museum (Natural History).

Published in hardback and paperback

ISBN 0 948881 00 3 (hardback edition)
ISBN 0 948881 01 1 (paperback edition)

British Library Cataloguing in Publication Data
   Docherty, James
   Growing Up: a guide for children and parents.
   1. Puberty—Juvenile literature
   I. Title
   612'.661   QP84.4

Printed in England by Waterlow Limited, Dunstable
a member of the BPCC Group

The publishers gratefully acknowledge the contribution of the following individuals and organisations:

- for photographs taken specially for this book:
Joe Bulaitis (pages 12-15, 18-23, 25, 27, 30-33, 37, 42-45, 49-53, 55, 68-69, 70, 90, 95, 100-101, etc.)
Brian Harris (cover; pages 4, 16-17, etc.)
Maureen O'Connell MD, BS (pages 64-67, etc.)
Robert Taylor (pages 57, 58 top, 61-63, etc.)
Michael Townshend (pages 9, 11)
R. H. Whitaker FRCS (pages 38 top row, 40 left)

- for original artwork:
George Hayhurst (pages 13, 30-33, 42-45, 48-53, 57-58, 61-63, etc.)

- for special services, assistance and advice:
Adam Rouilly Ltd;
British Museum (Natural History);
Professor Ian Craft, Humana Hospital, Wellington, London;
Ms Michele Elliott, Director, Kidscape;
International Planned Parenthood Federation;
Islington Green Secondary School; Islington Sixth Form Centre;
Dr Werner Lansburgh;
National Society for the Prevention of Cruelty to Children;
Mr R. H. Whitaker, Addenbrooke's Hospital, Cambridge;
Dr Alan Wootliff, Spitalfields Health Centre, London

- for permission to reproduce photographs, etc.:
Lennart Nilssen (pages 34, 35, 53 top/bottom right, 59, 60; page 35 from Behold Man, others from A Child is Born, both published by Faber & Faber)
Adam Rouilly Ltd (fetuses pages 61-63); The Bridgeman Art Library (page 73 centre left); Charing Cross & Westminster Medical School (page 58 bottom); Ian Craft FRCS, MRCOG (page 56); W. J. Cunliffe FRCP, Leeds Dermatological Research Foundation/Roche Products Ltd (page 41 top); Daily Telegraph Colour Library/Space Frontiers (page 73 bottom right); Robert Estall (page 73 top left); John Hillelsen Agency (page 57 bottom); Controller of Her Majesty's Stationery Office—Crown copyright (page 97); Michael Holford (page 73 top right); The National Gallery, London—reproduction by courtesy of The Trustees (page 73 centre right); National Society for the Prevention of Cruelty to Children (page 93); St George's Hospital Medical School, London (page 54 bottom right); J. Sainsbury plc—copyright (page 102); Tate Gallery, London (page 73 bottom left)

- for technical services:
Aragorn Colour Reproductions; JDM Color Labs Ltd;
KWT Printing Services Ltd

The Royal Society of Medicine

a guide for children and parents by
Dr James Docherty

with a foreword by
Lord Rea of Eskdale M D

modus books

This seven-month-old fetus, many times life size, is a dramatic feature in the Hall of Human Biology at the Natural History Museum; this exhibition, which opened in 1977, has many thousands of visitors each year, most of them schoolchildren.

Foreword

Not very many years ago sex was approved and sanctioned only within marriage. This view is regarded as out of date by many young people today. About three in ten marriages end in divorce, and cohabitation is now recognised in law. About one birth in six is outside marriage and about one in seven is to mothers under 18. Sexual partners change more frequently and sexually transmitted diseases are an increasing public health problem.

Over the past three generations the onset of puberty has become much earlier and the average age of marriage later. A century ago the average girl reached menstruation at about 16 years and was quite likely to be married and pregnant by 17 or 18; she passed from childhood to womanhood in a year or two. Today the average girl reaches menstruation at 13 but will not marry until 23 or later; boys reach puberty later, but will also marry later, than girls.

This decade or more before settling down is one that should be an enjoyable and a very positive experience, but too often it is beset with difficult or painful emotional and physical problems.

Doctors are often asked for advice and help at this stage, although too many teenagers suffer in silence because they fear that their general practitioner may be unsympathetic, or be associated with their parents with whom they may not be able to communicate easily. Any attempt to tackle the causes of these doubts and difficulties is therefore very welcome.

To develop a healthy and well informed attitude to sexuality in the widest sense is the first step towards more responsible and caring behaviour between people of different sexes. This attitude should be based on an accurate knowledge and understanding of the anatomy and physiology of reproduction: the 'facts of life'.

GROWING UP has been produced with this in mind. The book has quite a new approach. The content is aimed particularly at those approaching puberty and adolescence but the text is more thorough than usual. The special appeal and effectiveness of the book, however, is its striking visual representation with the use of dozens of real-life colour photographs.

We believe this book is unique and will be a very popular and valuable aid to children and their parents in providing reliable and accurate information in a very natural way.

Nicolas Rea

THE LORD REA OF ESKDALE, MD, MRCGP, is the President of the Section of General Practice of the Royal Society of Medicine. For some years a Research Fellow in Pædiatrics in Lagos, Nigeria, and later Lecturer in Social Medicine at St Thomas's Hospital Medical School, he is now a family doctor in Kentish Town, London. Lord Rea regularly takes his seat in the House of Lords, where he speaks on a wide range of medical and social issues.

to your parents

The purpose of GROWING UP is very simple: to explain to children who have not yet reached adolescence exactly what to expect when they do, and to help them prepare for the many physical and emotional changes to come.

Concerned parents who would like to give their children the best possible help in preparing for adolescence have to make some difficult decisions. For example: what and how much information should the children be given, when and how should they be given it, what role should be taken by the parents and the school, what materials should be used?

● **the great debate**

There is a school of thought which sees childhood as a time of true sexlessness, innocent and carefree, which must be protected and preserved for as long as possible. It advocates censorship of sex education materials and tight control of teachers because, it argues, conventional sex education starts too soon, debases traditional moral and family values, unhealthily emphasises the physical at the expense of the emotional and moral, and encourages immorality and promiscuity. It judges existing sex education material to be frequently amoral and brutally explicit, and many sex educators to be self-appointed 'sexperts' whose normality and motives are questionable.

Another school of thought starts from the understanding that children have a powerful natural sexuality which needs to be recognised and respected; that their curiosity is healthy and not prurient; and that by the time they are approaching puberty they have not only a need for but also a right to uncensored information about what lies ahead.

You have no doubt already made up your own minds about which of these attitudes is yours and, from even the most cursory glance, you can see which is favoured in this book.

● **the scope of the book**

In an ideal world, the best place to learn about sex would be in the ideal home and the best educator would be the ideal parent. In the real world, however, this is rarely so. With the best intentions, many parents feel inhibited and unable to take on the job of teaching their children themselves, or at least to do so unaided. Many will wish to use an authoritative book as an aid; many more will decide to leave it all to a book, or to the school.

On the assumption that you are evaluating GROWING UP as an aid, you will want to know exactly where it stands and what ground it covers.

It starts from the proposition that children should be as well-informed as possible, and well in advance of puberty. The first menstruation or wet-dream or crush can be quite an alarming experience if it is not expected and understood.

If the journey to adulthood emerges as a series of unpleasant surprises, shrouded in a pall of mystery and embarrassed silence, the adolescent years can become an ordeal, a time of anxiety, depression and unhappiness to be endured until at last it is over. If on the other hand the way ahead is clearly mapped and well understood, with positive support at hand whenever it is needed, adolescence will be looked forward to as an exciting and rewarding adventure.

Within specific limits, GROWING UP therefore covers every topic which the older child is likely to find useful. It deals with the physiology of growth and reproduction; it explains and illustrates the physical facts of coitus, conception, pregnancy and birth; it examines the new emotional experiences of adolescence; it answers the main questions which girls and boys ask about the private experiences of menstruation, ejaculation and masturbation; and it discusses their growing responsibility for looking after themselves and their growing obligations to others.

- **adult topics**

  Most books which cover this ground thoroughly also devote even more space to such matters as love-making and sexual orientation, contraception and sexually transmitted diseases. We have taken the view that since these matters are outside the immediate future practical experience of the great majority of children, they are best dealt with in a separate book. (The second, companion volume to GROWING UP will deal with these adult subjects.)

  However, all children encounter the adult world vicariously every day in countless ways through normal social life, in books and magazines and the mass media, and so on. They are curious, and it is unrealistic to suppose that curiosity disappears by being ignored. If children are not given straight simple answers about things to do with sex in the same way that they are about other matters, they will find out by other means—and often by means of which you would not approve. Ignorance is *not* bliss: ignorance breeds anxiety and harmful misinformation.

  The principal areas of adult sexual experience and problems are therefore touched upon in the text (notably in the last section Life Ahead), but only quite briefly, and the most important relevant words which children may encounter are included in the extensive glossary.

- **the text**

  Within these limits, GROWING UP is wholly frank in both text and pictures. The intention is always to give factual information, to correct *mis*information, to illuminate areas often left dark, and to provide reassurance. The text contains an unusual amount of detailed facts, but you will nevertheless find that it is well within the capacity of older children (say 12-14) with enquiring minds.

  Many parents as well as children have difficulty with the vocabulary of sex and the body. The popular or slang words can be embarrassing and confusing (the terms 'egg' and 'seed', for example, may conjure up wholly misleading visions of chicken eggs and plant seeds). Apart from a few common words (breast, womb, testicle, sperm, foreskin), only the correct terms are used in this book. It is worth persevering with these, even if they feel a bit awkward to begin with, because they are neutral and unambiguous. (Correct pronunciation is indicated in the glossary.)

  The book is organised so that it is easy to find specific information but also easy to ignore anything which is not of immediate interest (it is helpful for children to know that information is available when it is wanted).

  There is one particular difficulty about writing a book of this kind which seems to be practically insuperable: in the interests of clarity and brevity it is necessary to simplify, but simplifications are unscientific. You will find such imprecise words as 'some', 'many', 'most', 'usually' and 'on average' scattered through the text, but there are also many unqualified statements. Except in the cases where I am absolutely emphatic, I ask you to take for granted that there is probably an exception to practically every bald statement. Statistics, too, are simplified: one cannot usefully talk of the average number of births per mother being 2.3!

- **advice**

  The text concentrates on facts: advice is given only sparingly and is confined to matters of responsibilities and obligations. It is also—as you might expect of a doctor—offered from a medical viewpoint rather than a religious or moralistic one.

  The attitudes of young people are very much influenced and shaped by the moral beliefs of the particular family, religion and community in which they grow up.

  It is not my purpose in any way to try to influence or change those beliefs.

  However, the world in which we were brought up was very different from the one in which our children are now growing up. The quality of the changes, be they for better or worse, is not in question here; but it is necessary to recognise that they are quite profound, both in the overall fabric of society and in patterns of family life. These matters are not emphasised in the book, but neither are they ignored.

- **the pictures**

  Finally, a few words about the pictures which form such an important part of the book. We have chosen the unusual course of using photographs of real people in the anatomy pictures simply because diagrams of the conventional type can be very confusing and misleading.

  Four sequences of colour pictures are particularly important: the female and male sex organs (pages 30-33 and 42-45), the sequence of events in coitus (pages 49-53) and the development of the baby-to-be through the nine months of pregnancy (pages 57-63). We have tried not only to portray the internal anatomy as clearly as possible but also to convey something of its intrinsic beauty, which is captured so well in the photographs by Lennart Nilssen (pages 35, 53, 59 and 60).

  From the decision to use colour photographs as the basis for the pictures of the internal anatomy, it was only a short step to deciding to illustrate the external anatomy in the same way. The cheerful naturalness of the many families, couples and individuals in these pictures conveys a message which will be reassuring to a great many young people.

- **for young children**

  Children's questions about sex come out of the blue when you least expect them. Once you are familiar with the book, you may well find it useful at such moments. Even quite young children will be well able to appreciate the pictures and will accept and absorb the information in them without embarrassment. Indeed, the first two sections of GROWING UP have been designed to be used as a picture book for young children.

JAMES N. DOCHERTY, MB, ChB, DPH, received his medical training in Scotland. He is now a family doctor in London, and also works in a large teaching hospital. A Fellow of the Royal Society of Medicine, he has been a member of the London Executive Council and other committees of the National Health Service. Both as a doctor and as a teacher of students, he has had long experience of young people and their problems.

growth

'It's a girl!'.... 'It's a boy!'.... Those were probably the very first words to be spoken over you when you were born.

Boy, girl.... man, woman.... he, she.... sister, brother.... daughter, son.... mother, father.... These are some of the first words we learn and all of them identify the **sex** (or **gender**) of the person: **male** or **female**. This division into two sexes is the most important thing about the human race.

Each one of us exists only because at the time of our creation we had two parents: one female and one male. Without a mother and a father we could not have been born. We are all born at a particular moment in time and at a particular place in the world: we are born into a community as well as a family. From our parents we inherit our main physical and mental characteristics—our shape, colour, features and so on—as well as, in another sense, our language and religion. The community we live in takes responsibility for our education and gives us our traditions, nationality and laws.

All these things shape and control our lives in very important ways, but if there is a single *most* important fact in our lives it is the sex we are born with. The natural process which determines our sex is as random as the toss of a coin—heads or tails, male or female. We never know the moment at which the choice is made, and the choice itself remains nature's secret until we are born. But from that moment on, the course of our lives is largely bound by the choice that nature has made for us.

Everyone therefore needs to understand just what sex is, and why it is, and what it means for each of us in our bodies and in our minds. That is why sex plays such an important part in GROWING UP.

We are now going to look at the main changes which take place in our bodies as we grow up. We shall look first at the growth of both sexes from baby to adult (pages 10-23), and then in detail at what happens as a girl grows into a woman (pages 24-35) and a boy into a man (pages 36-47).

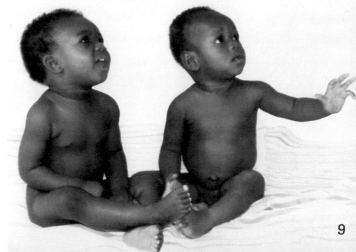

One of these 10-month-old baby cousins is a girl and the other is a boy. Can you be sure which is which? Turn the page to find out.

baby to adult

Growing up means developing from baby to adult: from baby girl to woman, from baby boy to man.

Very young babies look much alike. Their clothes may tell you if they are boys or girls, but not their faces, their voices or the shape of their bodies. Even when they are wearing only nappies, it is still impossible to tell for certain: both have **nipples** on their chests and both have a **navel** (belly button). It is only when they are naked that the difference between the sexes becomes obvious.

The baby girl has a narrow opening at the **crotch** (that is, the area between the legs at the bottom of the belly). This opening is called the **vulva**. The open end of the tube through which she **urinates** (passes the liquid waste called **urine** out of the body) is just inside the vulva. This tube is called the **urethra**.

The baby boy also has an opening at the crotch for urinating, but it takes a different form: his urethra comes out through a short tube of flesh projecting outside the body. This is called the **penis**. Below the penis hangs a bag of skin, wrinkled and a little darker than the skin around, called the **scrotum**. Inside the scrotum are two small round organs called **testicles**.

Most young girls and boys find out that rubbing the vulva or penis gives them a feeling of pleasure. Just because these parts are the only differences between the sexes which can be seen and touched, most young children are very interested in them. This curiosity is natural and quite harmless.

The organ in which urine collects and is stored before urinating is called the **bladder**. The opening between the buttocks through which we **defecate** (pass the solid waste called **feces** out of the body) is called the **anus**. The anus and the bladder are the same for both sexes.

Apart from the differences which you can see, there are other differences between boys and girls *inside* their bodies, and we shall look at these later.

PLEASE READ THIS
All the way through this book you will find a lot of medical and other terms which are probably new to you. When they appear for the first time they are usually in bold type (like this: **crotch**). All of these terms are included in the **glossary** on pages 74-80, where you will find a short definition and also the correct pronunciation. You can also consult the **index** on pages 110-111 to find all the references to any particular subject which may interest you.

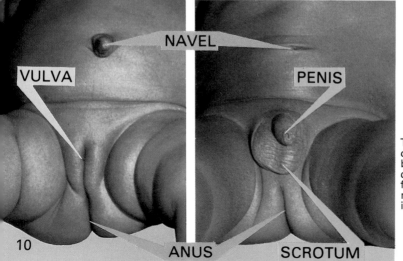

VULVA NAVEL PENIS

ANUS SCROTUM

Now that the bab are standing up course you can which is which— only because crotch is not cover

These are the three outside parts of the body by which you can tell a baby girl from a baby boy. The names are explained in the text.

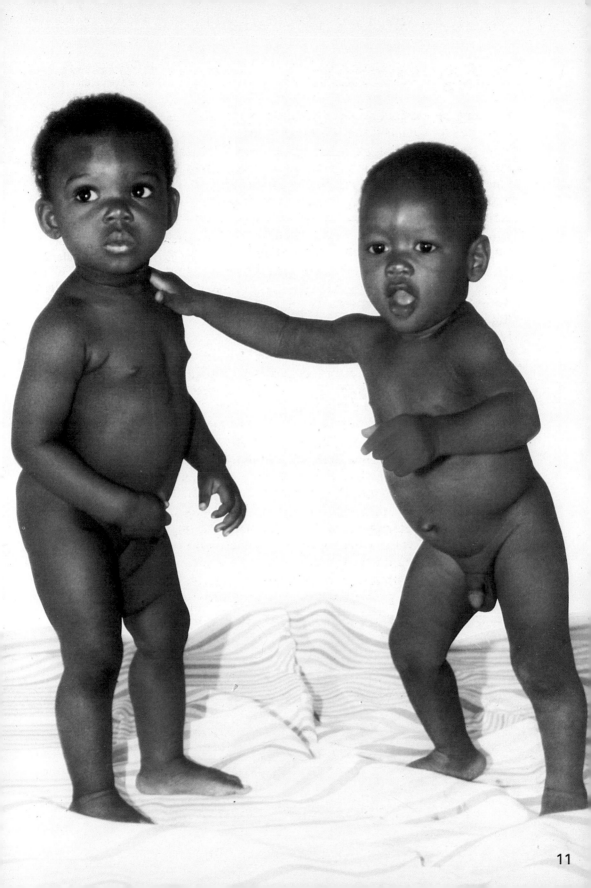

A baby is a complete human being when it is born. All the bones of the skeleton are already there, and so are all the organs: the brain, eyes, heart, lungs, stomach, bladder, and so on.

It takes on average about 19 years—around 7000 days or about a quarter of the average life span—for the baby to become an adult, and the process of growing up is going on all this time. Growth is fairly even and smooth year by year (although a few organs grow more quickly than the others) until some time early in the second half of this period.

There then begins a series of special changes in the body which mark the end of childhood and will lead finally to adulthood and **maturity**. This stage in life, which every one of us goes through, is called **adolescence** and lasts several years. Any young person going through these years may be called an **adolescent** (teenager means much the same thing).

The changes which begin at adolescence are controlled by **hormones** which the body now begins to make in several **glands**. The body makes many substances for itself (blood, saliva, sweat and tears are some we can see), and *hormones* are special substances which control the development of the physical shape, appearance and activity of the body. *Glands* are organs which produce hormones and some of the other substances which the body needs for special purposes. The hormones which control growth and start the main changes of adolescence are produced by the **pituitary gland**, which is situated behind the eyes and under the brain.

The growth in height and weight which has been going on all through childhood continues as adolescence begins, but then for a year or two it speeds up. This is called the **growth spurt** or **height spurt** and comes about two years earlier in girls than in boys: usually from about $10\frac{1}{2}$ to 12 years of age for girls, and from about $12\frac{1}{2}$ to $14\frac{1}{2}$ for boys. It is very marked in some young people and hardly noticeable in others.

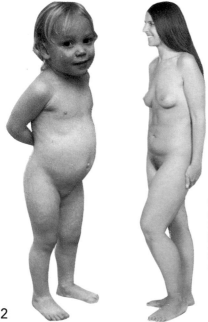

On the right you can see how the ave female and male bodies change as develop from baby to adult. The childh years (when not much is changing ex height) are shown at four-year inter (2, 6, 10), and the adolescent years at year intervals (10, 12, 14, 16, 18). The s of the average growth spurt is shown by two darkest shades of green for girls brown for boys. Note that a girl's gro spurt starts about two years before a bo The elder daughter of this family is 15 is already an adolescent, but her you brother, who is 13, has not yet sta

When a baby is born its head is about one-quarter of its height from top to toe. By adulthood the head has become only one-eighth of the height. This is because of the brain, which at birth is much larger in proportion to its adult size than any other organ in the body.

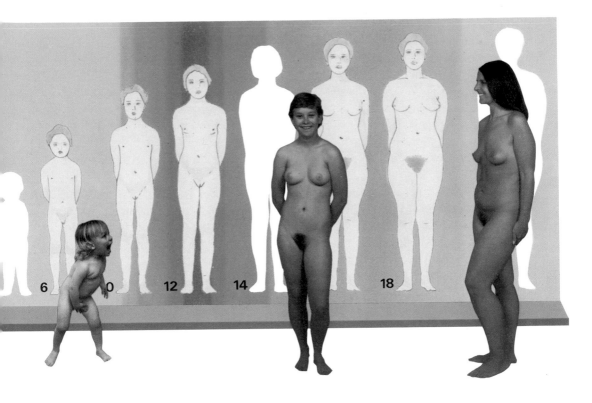

6   0   12   14   18

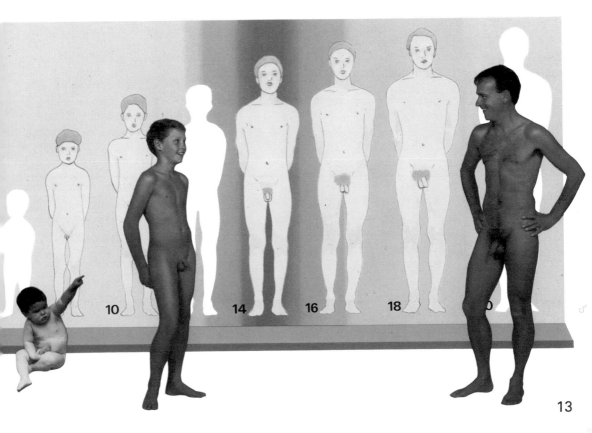

10   14   16   18   0

Adolescence starts when the first important differences in shape and appearance between males and females begin to develop. These differences will become more and more noticeable each year until maturity is reached.

In girls the hips grow wider, and in boys the shoulders. While boys become more muscular, girls begin to develop **breasts** and the flesh thickens on their thighs and hips so that these become rounder. In both sexes the nipples and the **areolas** round them become much larger. Many boys also briefly show signs of developing breasts, but these disappear after a few months; some may feel discomfort in their nipples for a time.

In both sexes, hair begins to grow around the crotch and **groin** (where the legs join the trunk or torso) and in the armpits. Hair at the groin—around the vulva or penis and scrotum—has a special name: **pubic hair**. Most boys and some girls also begin to grow hair on the face (**facial hair**), on the legs and maybe on the chest and belly (**body hair**)—although this often does not develop until much later on. In due course, too, the boy's Adam's apple grows; as a result, his voice becomes deeper and stronger and may 'break' noticeably.

In adolescent girls, the position of the vulva gradually moves downwards between the legs a little. In adolescent boys, the testicles grow to four or five centimetres long, the scrotum enlarges, and the penis grows longer and thicker.

Another change which adolescents will find is that they now **sweat** more than before—particularly in the armpits, around the crotch and between the toes. The sweat may now have a strong smell, but this is quite natural and can be washed away with soap and water.

In both boys and girls, too, the skin becomes less soft and smooth during adolescence. While this is happening, it is quite usual for pimples or spots to appear on the face, neck and back for a time. These spots are called **acne**. (There is more about this on page 40.)

Not only do our bodies change in shape and appearance as we grow up, but certain parts now begin to work for the first time: these are the parts which are going to be needed in adult life for making babies. In both the sexes, nature's purpose is to make the body able to produce babies: that is, to **reproduce**. The girl grows into a woman who can become a mother, the boy grows into a man who can become a father.

Developing the power of **reproduction**—achieving sexual maturity—is the most important part of adolescence, and the period during which this is happening has a special name: **puberty**. Puberty comes during the early part of adolescence, which means that young people reach sexual maturity a few years before they become fully adult in other ways.

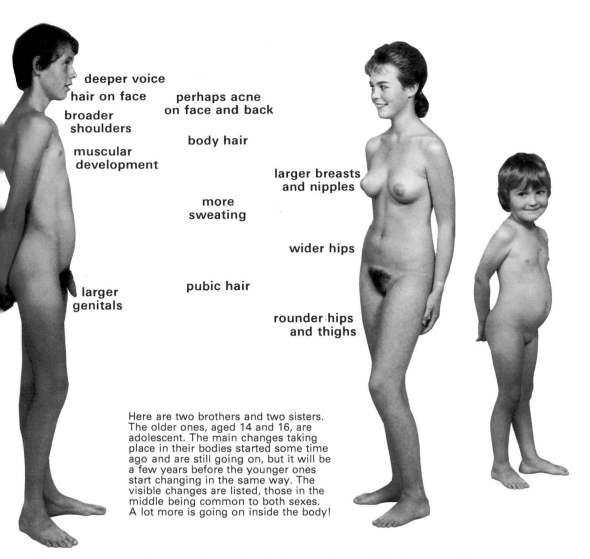

deeper voice

hair on face

perhaps acne
on face and back

broader
shoulders

muscular
development

body hair

larger breasts
and nipples

more
sweating

wider hips

larger
genitals

pubic hair

rounder hips
and thighs

Here are two brothers and two sisters. The older ones, aged 14 and 16, are adolescent. The main changes taking place in their bodies started some time ago and are still going on, but it will be a few years before the younger ones start changing in the same way. The visible changes are listed, those in the middle being common to both sexes. A lot more is going on inside the body!

There are several organs in the body designed specially for reproduction, and these are the parts which begin to grow rapidly and to work only from puberty. They are called the **sex organs** or **genitals**.

The organs which can be seen (the breasts and vulva in a woman; the penis, scrotum and testicles in a man) are called the *external* sex organs. Those inside the body, which have all been present since birth but do not begin developing until now, are called the *internal* sex organs.

Our bodies are made up of millions upon millions of tiny 'building blocks' called **cells**. There are special cells for reproduction, called **gametes** (or **germ-cells**), which are made by the female and male sex organs. No baby can be created unless the gamete produced by the mother, called an **ovum** (or egg), is united with the gamete produced by the father, called a **sperm** (or seed). Both these gametes have to be able to unite when they meet. If they can, we say they are **fertile**; and when they unite we say that the sperm **fertilises** the ovum. The fertilised ovum will eventually grow into a baby.

The first signs of puberty which you are likely to notice are different for girls and boys. If you are a girl, the first sign is the development of the breasts, usually starting around the age of 11. If you are a boy, it is the appearance of the first pubic hairs, usually around the age of 12 (the testicles have started to grow a few months earlier, but you are unlikely to notice this at first). In girls the height spurt starts shortly before the breasts appear, and in boys soon after the first pubic hairs appear.

You can also tell when the internal sex organs begin to work, usually a year or two later. When a girl begins to produce *ova* (ova is the plural of ovum), she also begins to **menstruate**; and when a boy begins to produce sperms, he also begins to **ejaculate**. **Menstruation** results in a small amount of blood (which is discharged naturally inside the body) flowing from a girl's vulva every four weeks or so; and **ejaculation** is a small amount of special liquid called **semen** which is discharged from a boy's penis from time to time.

These new events may seem strange at first, even though you are expecting them, but they quickly become a natural part of life. (There is much more on the sex organs, menstruation and ejaculation later in the book.)

For most children, adolescence starts at about 11 or 12 years, and comes to an end at about 18 or 19 years. Girls on average start two years earlier than boys. However, there are big differences between individual girls and boys in the time at which adolescence begins (for some as early as 9 or 10, for others as late as 14 or 15), and in the speed at which they develop.

It can therefore happen (particularly among girls around 12 and boys around 14) that some have already completed puberty before others of exactly the same age have even started. This may be alarming for the 'early developer' and very frustrating for the 'late developer', but there is nothing unusual or abnormal about either: starting earlier than average is just as common and normal as starting later.

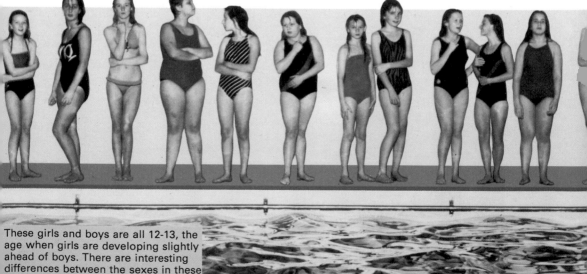

These girls and boys are all 12-13, the age when girls are developing slightly ahead of boys. There are interesting differences between the sexes in these two groups—can you see any?

The timing and pattern of your own puberty and adolescence is something that you inherit from your parents. There is nothing that you can do to speed it up or slow it down—or indeed change it in any way—and there is no need at all to worry about it.

Some adolescents spend a lot of time worrying about the appearance of their bodies. They look at their friends and wonder if they themselves are too short or too tall, too fat or too thin. Perhaps they fear that they are plain or ugly. They may see others naked, perhaps another girl with bigger breasts or another boy with a thicker penis: they wonder if their own sex organs are too small or too big, or if they are somehow not 'normal'.

The world seems to be full of people with pale complexions who want to be darker or are dark but want to be fairer, with straight hair who want it curly or with curly hair who want it straight, who think their nose is too small or their feet are too big, and so on. The details of the appearance of your body are all things that you inherit, and there is little or nothing you can do to change any of them (except perhaps your weight). The only practical thing to do is to stop worrying about them!

Girls and boys are naturally sensitive about the changes in their bodies, and sometimes they feel that everyone must be looking at them and talking about them. This is just imagination at work. It may help you to remember that, while the changes now taking place in your body are private to you, *nothing* that is happening to you is unique: it has all happened to millions upon millions of other people before, and it is all happening to millions of other young people at this very moment. You need never feel embarrassed about any of the natural processes of growing up.

The three main ways in which our bodies differ on the outside—as the pictures below show well—are in size, in shape and in skin colour, and we are now going to look at each of these in turn.

Size means height (sometimes called **stature**) and weight. Except for a short time during the growth spurt (which we looked at on pages 12-13), males are on average taller than females. The difference is very little in babies but increases to an average of about 13 centimetres in adulthood.

This is shown clearly on the chart on the facing page. You can also see that the average height for adult women and men is about 162cms and 175cms respectively, and that about half of all women and men are in the ranges 159-165cms and 172-179cms.

During the growth spurt, girls and boys usually increase their height by between 6cms and 12cms each year. Growth in height slows down almost to a standstill on average by the age of 16 in girls and 18 in boys, but both grow a further few millimetres in the next four or five years.

Babies weigh on average between 3 and $3\frac{1}{2}$ kilograms at birth (male babies about 200 grams more than females) and adult males are generally heavier than adult females of the same height. Differences in weight, however, are very much greater than differences in height; this is partly because of the differences in our natural shape and partly because our weight is so much affected by what we eat. (There is more about these two subjects on pages 20-21 and 100-101 respectively.)

You can check your weight in this way: multiply your height in metres by itself and then divide your weight in kilos by this figure. If the result is between 18 and 25 your weight is within the normal range. (Thus, someone 1.6 metres tall weighing 55 kilos divides 55 by 2.56, result 21.5.)

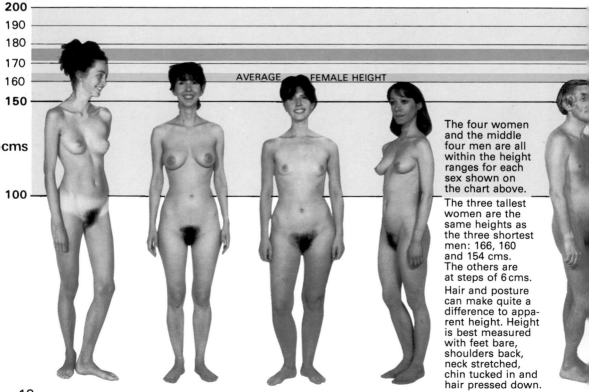

200
190
180
170
160
150

AVERAGE   FEMALE HEIGHT

cms

100

The four women and the middle four men are all within the height ranges for each sex shown on the chart above.

The three tallest women are the same heights as the three shortest men: 166, 160 and 154 cms. The others are at steps of 6 cms.

Hair and posture can make quite a difference to apparent height. Height is best measured with feet bare, shoulders back, neck stretched, chin tucked in and hair pressed down.

On this chart, red is for girls and blue is for boys, and the *thick* line in each colour is the *average* growth curve. About half of all girls and boys fall within the band limited by the *medium dotted* lines above and below the average (this band is the shaded area), and nearly all the rest are within the outer band limited by the *thin dotted* lines.

You can also clearly see the growth spurt (explained on page 12) for girls and boys, and the period between 11½ and 14 when girls overtake boys in average height.

You can use this chart to find out how tall you are likely to be when you are adult. Mark the point where your present height (horizontal lines) crosses your age (vertical lines) and see if you are on the average line (the *thick* one) or above or below it. Then mark the same relative position (on, above or below the average) on the 19 age line, and read off the height you will probably be.

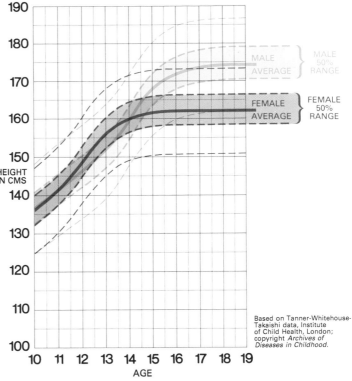

Based on Tanner-Whitehouse-Takaishi data, Institute of Child Health, London; copyright *Archives of Diseases in Childhood.*

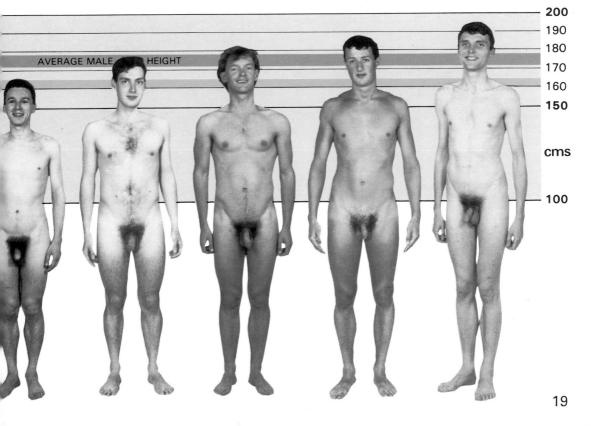

19

During adolescence our body takes on its adult shape or **physique**. This is the shape we have inherited, and is fixed by the natural shape of our **frame** or skeleton, and the natural distribution of flesh (fat and muscle) on it.

Scientists say there are three extreme types of basic physique, which are shown in cartoon form below. They are:

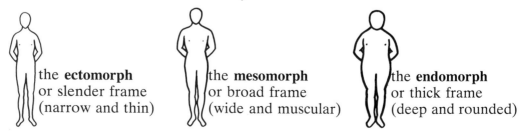

the **ectomorph** or slender frame (narrow and thin)

the **mesomorph** or broad frame (wide and muscular)

the **endomorph** or thick frame (deep and rounded)

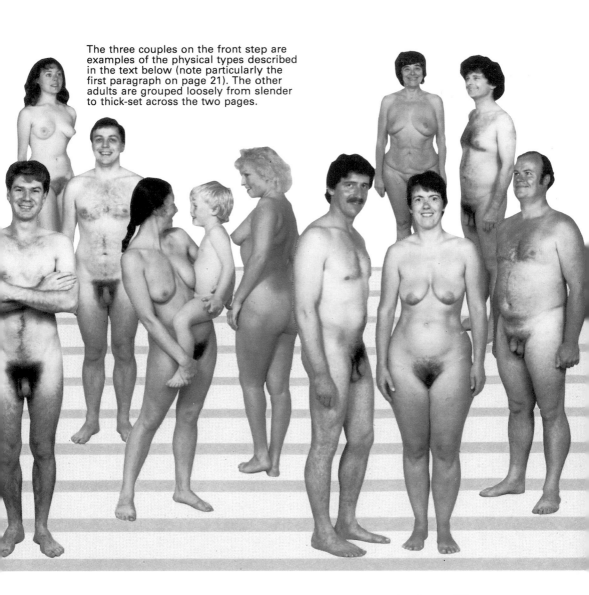

The three couples on the front step are examples of the physical types described in the text below (note particularly the first paragraph on page 21). The other adults are grouped loosely from slender to thick-set across the two pages.

Everybody has a certain amount of all these components in them. The vast majority of people are not extremes (like the cartoons) but mixtures, with one component more pronounced than the others—like the men and women on these pages. On average, there are more women than men within the endomorph range.

What and how much we eat, and the amount and type of exercise we take, all affect our weight and our shape but will not alter our *basic* physique. Thus, endomorph types who eat too little do not become ectomorphs, they simply become thinner endomorphs; and although ectomorphs have thin frames, they can be quite fat if they eat too much.

Remember that physique is quite independent of height: all ectomorph, mesomorph and endomorph types can be tall, short or of average height.

The third main external difference we can see is skin colour.

Most people in this book have the pale, pinkish skin called 'white' because most of those photographed happen to have white skins, and not because we were particularly looking for white skins to photograph. In fact, in the human race as a whole only about one person in five has 'white' skin. The other four have skins called by such names as 'yellow', 'brown' and 'black'. These are handy labels, but very inaccurate: many 'white' people, for example, have darker skins than many 'black'.

We have now looked at the three ways in which our bodies (regardless of sex) differ visibly: in size, in shape and in skin colour. There are also, however, three main ways of grouping humankind in physical terms: by gender, by shape, and by **race** or **ethnic group**. There are five main ethnic groups (see the bottom of this page) and several much smaller ones.

These groupings are based on physical characteristics such as colour of skin and eyes and type of features, hair and blood. In some of these there may be bigger differences between people within a group than between people of different groups—and often cultural differences are more important than physical ones. Confusion arises because such names as 'black' and 'white' are used to describe not only skin colour but also racial or ethnic origin.

Over the centuries countless millions of people in all the ethnic groups have migrated to other parts of the world, and have then intermixed and intermarried. As a result many millions of people today are of **mixed race**: that is, their parents belong to different ethnic groups. Another result is that most societies are now, like ours, **multi-ethnic** or **multi-cultural**. The intermixing continues, increases and cannot be reversed. Very gradually, although not without difficulties, the old barriers are breaking down.

Unlike the other physical differences we have looked at, skin colour is literally skin deep: the way in which our bodies and minds grow and work is the same in all human beings, whatever our colour and wherever we live.

AMERICAN INDIAN
various parts of North and South America

AFRICAN
Africa South of the Sahara, Caribbean, parts of South America, etc.

EUROPEAN
Europe, North Africa, Middle East, North America, etc.

ASIAN
whole Indian sub-continent

FAR EASTERN
China, Japan, Mongolia, South East Asia, etc.

These are the five largest ethnic groups, arranged according to size. Each of the little black figures represents nearly 50 million people. The pictures show families from countries where most of the population belong to one of these groups. Of course, each ethnic group spans many countries, and many have several or all of the groups in their population.

The sixth family, with one outline figure, represents all the other ethnic groups, which are all very much smaller. The pictures are based on families depicted in posters from Austria, China, Colombia, Ghana, Indonesia and Pakistan. Can you work out how many people there are in each ethnic group, and which family comes from which country?

OTHERS
various parts of Australasia, etc.

Family planning posters by courtesy of the International Planned Parenthood Federation.

The women and men in this group represent all the main ethnic groups. All of them live in Britain, but their parents or grandparents came from China, South and West Africa, India, Jamaica, Puerto Rico, Lebanon and the Mediterranean. Some are of mixed race. They all have different skin colours, but these are only a few of the great range of different shades in the world: the rest are represented by the two silhouettes, which you can colour with your imagination!

girl to woman

Most species on earth have two sexes, and in all these the female produces ova. In many species (like the birds and fishes) these ova will grow into eggs even if they are not fertilised by sperms from a male. In others, however (like the mammals, which include human beings), an ovum will not grow into a baby unless it is first fertilised.

Nature gives the female the most important role in human life: to carry and nourish the new life inside her from the moment of fertilisation until the full-grown baby is ready to be born, and to feed it in the early months of life. The time from fertilisation to birth—about nine months—is called **pregnancy**, and during this period the mother-to-be is said to be **pregnant**.

Of course, not all women have babies. For one reason or another, some do not want to, some want to but do not have the opportunity, and some are not able to. In Britain, eight or nine out of every ten women do become mothers, and most mothers have two babies, although many have only one and others have three or more.

Of the women who do have babies, most are married but many are not. In other words, a baby's mother and father do not need to be husband and wife: marriage is usually a matter of religion, law, custom and choice, affecting the circumstances of having a baby, while of course the processes of fertilisation, pregnancy and birth are purely physical things. We will come back to this much later in the book (on page 106).

A great many women become pregnant but do not have a baby. Indeed, it is estimated that about half of all pregnancies fail, and come to an end naturally in what is called an **abortion** or **miscarriage**. Many babies are born before they are fully developed, and some of these **premature** babies die soon after they are born. Sometimes, too, babies may be born fully-grown but unable to breathe: these are called **still-born** babies.

There are many different reasons for miscarriages, premature births and still-births. Scientists and doctors are learning more all the time about the mysteries of fertilisation and pregnancy, and nowadays many women can be given medical help to enable their pregnancies to be successful.

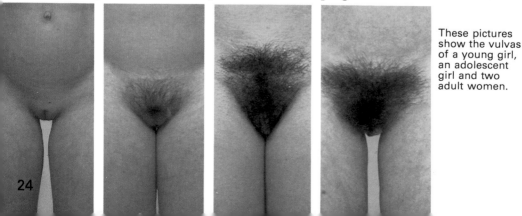

These pictures show the vulvas of a young girl, an adolescent girl and two adult women.

The years of your puberty and adolescence are going to be dominated by preparation for womanhood. In the next pages we are going to examine the female sex organs and learn how they work. Later in the book we will be looking in detail at what happens in your body during pregnancy and birth.

The first sign of puberty which you will see in your body is, as I have said, the beginning of the growth of the **breasts**. They will take about four years to grow to their adult size. The second sign is the appearance of pubic hair, which does not usually happen until six months or so after the breasts begin to appear, and which will then take about three years to develop.

The purpose of the breasts is to provide the milk which is the only food a baby needs for months after it is born. Each breast contains many small glands which make the milk, and many tubes which carry it to the nipple. A baby sucks on the nipple when it is being breast-fed.

During puberty the areola (the ring of darker skin round each nipple) becomes darker and much larger, and the nipples are now able to become **erect**. This means that they become quite hard when they are stimulated (by rubbing, for example, or by the baby sucking).

Many girls worry about the size and shape of their breasts (or **bosom**), and often about the fact that one breast may start to grow before the other, or grow to be a little different in size and shape from the other. This is very common. If this is the case with you, try to remember that you are certainly far more aware of it then anyone else. The great majority of other people will not notice it at all.

A lot of nonsense is talked about the size of the breasts. The fact is that breast size has no effect whatever on a woman's sexual ability and little effect on the ability of a mother to feed her baby.

The breasts usually enlarge during pregnancy, but the actual amount varies a lot. The length of time the breasts will produce milk to feed the baby also varies a lot—from a few weeks to a year or two. Human milk is different from cow's milk and contains just the right food for a young baby.

If a mother does not want to breast-feed her baby, or if her breasts do not produce milk, it must be bottle-fed with an artificial milk—although this is not quite as good as breast milk.

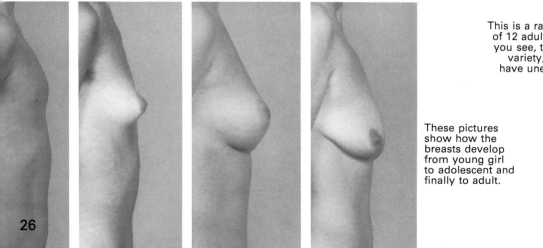

This is a random g of 12 adult womer you see, there is g variety, and se have uneven brea

These pictures show how the breasts develop from young girl to adolescent and finally to adult.

26

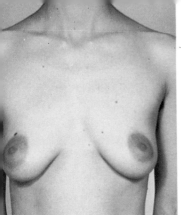
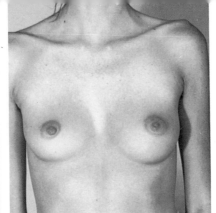
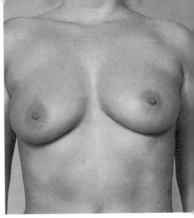

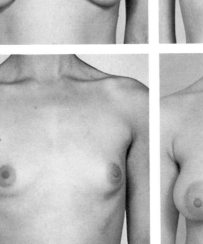
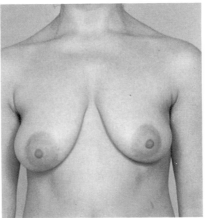
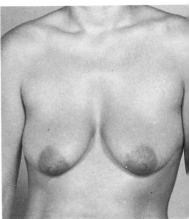

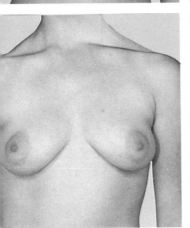
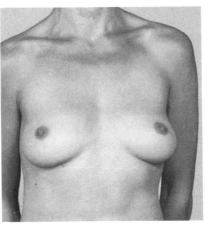
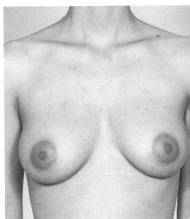

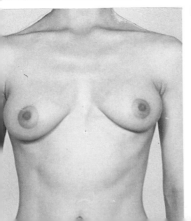
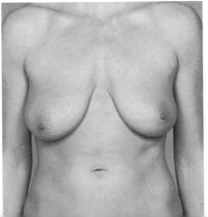
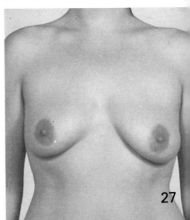

27

The other external sex organ, the vulva, has an inside as well as the outside. The outside has already been shown in the pictures on page 24 and the inside is shown on the facing page 29. At puberty, as the pubic hair begins to grow, the sides of the vulva (which are called the **labia**) become more thick and round. The word labia is Latin for lips, and in fact there are two pairs of these lips, called the **outer labia** and the **inner labia**.

If you pull the outer labia apart, you will find the darker, thinner and more petal-like pair of inner labia which protect the three parts which are just inside. These—as you can see on page 29—are the clitoris, the opening of the urethra and the entrance to the vagina.

The **clitoris** is almost all hidden inside the body and only the tip (called the **glans**) comes out into the vulva. This is very small and may itself be hidden by the **clitoral hood**, which is formed by the inner labia where they join at the top of the vulva. The clitoris swells and becomes erect when a woman is sexually stimulated. It is very sensitive and if it is rubbed it produces feelings of pleasure.

The **vagina** is the tube-like passage which joins the vulva to one of the most important internal sex organs: the **womb**, where a baby grows before it is born. The vagina (which is sometimes also called simply the **female organ**) is made of soft and delicate tissue and muscles, and is eight or nine centimetres long. It is normally quite narrow, but it can stretch easily.

The entrance from the vulva to the vagina may be partly blocked by a membrane (that is, a piece of very thin skin) which is called the **hymen**. The hymen varies a lot from one girl to another: the membrane may be tough or weak, the hole in it may be small or big, and some girls are even born without one. During childhood the hymen may stretch and open simply from natural exercise.

In the two central pictures you see clearly all the parts of the vu mentioned in the text above. N the position of the three openi (orifices): the entrance to the vag is between the urethra, whic also inside the vulva, and the ar There is even greater variety in shape of the vulva than the brea

Most girls have never looked carefully at their vulva, perhaps because they have been told not to. But it is helpful to know what it looks like, and there is nothing to be ashamed of. You can hold a mirror like the woman in the picture, and use your other hand to open the outer labia. If you can prop the mirror up somewhere, it is better to use both hands.

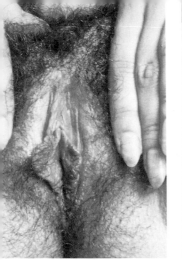
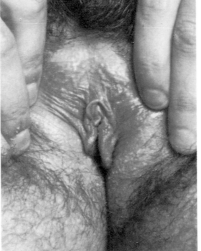
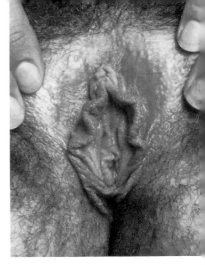

PUBIC HAIR

CLITORAL HOOD

CLITORIS

INNER LABIA

URETHRA

VAGINA

ANUS

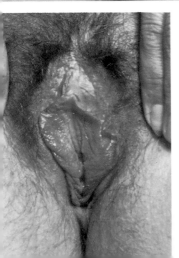
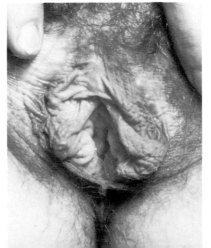
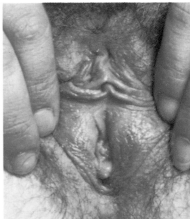

The most important sex organs in the female are the womb and the ovaries.

The **womb** (which is also called the **uterus**) has only one purpose: to protect and nourish the growing baby until it is ready to be born. The womb is hollow and when fully grown is only about eight centimetres long.

The **ovaries** are two glands which lie on each side of the womb. From puberty on, they make various **sex hormones** (which control a woman's sexual development and the process of menstruation), and they produce ova. From birth, each ovary has contained a large store of very tiny undeveloped ova; after puberty, some of these develop into ripe full-grown ova from time to time, as we shall see.

Entering the womb on each side near the top are two tubes called the **ovarian tubes** (or sometimes **fallopian tubes**). The open ends of these tubes have very fine and delicate tendrils, called **fimbriae**, which face the ovary, but are not actually connected to it. The womb has a narrow neck, called the **cervix**, at the lower end where it joins the top of the vagina. There is therefore a continuous passage from the open end of the ovarian tubes through the womb, cervix and vagina into the vulva.

In the pictures below and on the next three pages we look through the skin to see where all these organs are and how they are connected. Please take a few minutes now to look carefully through these pictures in sequence from 1 to 5, and to read the captions. There is a lot to look at, so you may find it helpful to go through the pictures more than once.

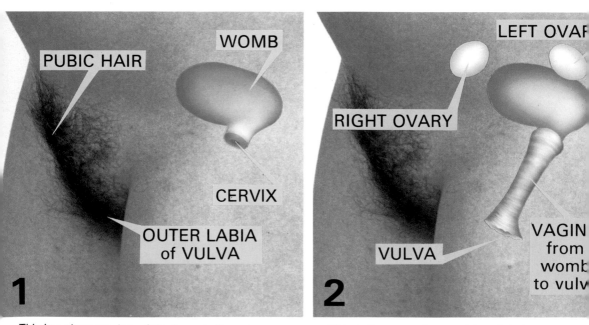

1

PUBIC HAIR

WOMB

CERVIX

OUTER LABIA of VULVA

This is a close-up view of the lower belly and crotch of the adult woman shown at the top of page 31. You can see the **pubic hair** which covers the **outer labia** of the **vulva**, and also the **womb** which sits inside the body. The **cervix** is the narrow entrance to the womb.

2

LEFT OVAR

RIGHT OVARY

VULVA

VAGIN from womb to vulv

This is the same view as picture 1, but with three more internal organs added: the two **ovaries** and the **vagina**. The ovaries sit on the left and right sides of the womb. The vagina is the tube which joins the cervix to the inside of the vulva.

The picture filling this page is an enlargement of the area outlined in black on the small full-length picture here on the right. For the sake of simplicity, the bones and the other internal organs are omitted in the big 'see-through' picture below, and only the internal sex organs and bladder are shown (This view of the body, half-front and half-side, is called three-quarter.)

In these pictures, and all the others where internal organs are shown, their locations and proportions are accurate but—to avoid confusion—their shapes are simplified and the colours are not real.

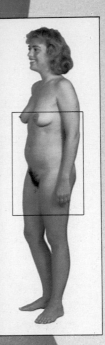

NAVEL

OVARIAN TUBES
entering womb

GROIN

URETHRA carrying
urine from bladder

BLADDER
storing urine

CLITORIS

INNER LABIA
of VULVA

3

ow the two **ovarian tubes** are added; one of the ends of these
ces the ovaries and the other end enters the womb. You can
so see the **clitoris** (the other internal sex organ) and the **inner
bia** of the vulva. All the internal sex organs are now in place.
nally, although these are *not* sex organs, the **bladder** and the
rethra (which opens into the vulva) are also included.

As on page 31, the pictures
filling these two pages are
enlargements of the area outlined in black on the small full-
length pictures on the right.
In the picture below, some of
the bones are shown. These
are: the **pelvis**, which stretches
across the body and forms the
hips; the **pubic bone**, which
is the front part of the pelvis
and lies just above the vulva;
and the beginning of the two
thigh-bones and the **spine**.
The female pelvis is wider and
shallower than the male one,
making it easier to support the
growing baby in the womb.

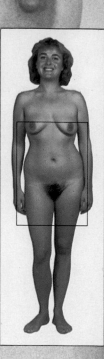

SPINE

PELVIS

OVARIAN TUBE

OVARY

BLADDER
(urethra not shown)

WOMB

VAGINA

4

PUBIC BONE
lying in front
of bladder

VULVA

We are looking at
the same organs as
we saw in picture 3,
but now we see them from the front. All that is
added are some of the bones, described above.
Notice how well the pelvis protects the womb.

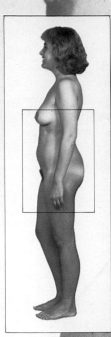

In the side view of the organs below, only one ovary and one ovarian tube are visible. Notice the cross-sections of the **pubic bone** and base of the **spine** (indicated only, not in detail) and how far the spine comes into the body. The position of the **anus** and the lower end of the **bowel** are also shown. You can now see clearly the three tubes which lead out of the body: the vagina in the middle, the urethra in front (both opening into the vulva) and the anus behind the vulva.

the organs and tubes marked
A → B → C → D   E
are the main parts of
a woman's sexual system

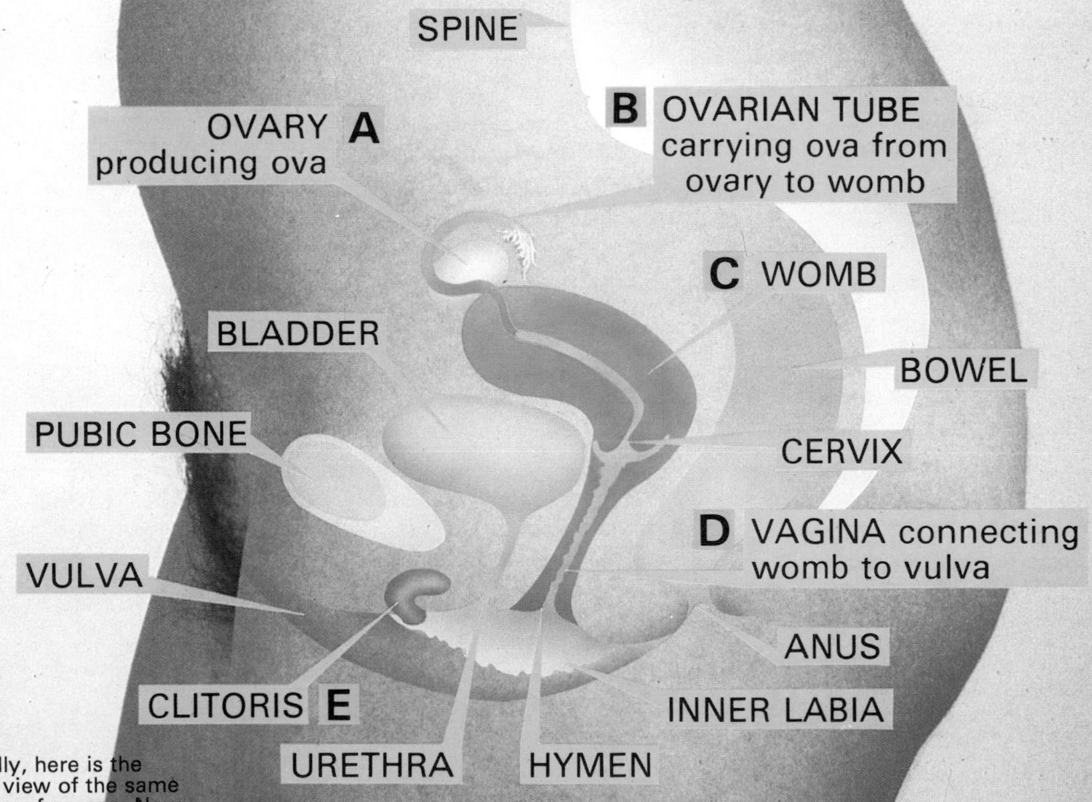

SPINE

OVARY **A**
producing ova

B OVARIAN TUBE
carrying ova from
ovary to womb

C WOMB

BLADDER

BOWEL

PUBIC BONE

CERVIX

D VAGINA connecting
womb to vulva

VULVA

ANUS

5

CLITORIS **E**

INNER LABIA

URETHRA   HYMEN

Finally, here is the
side view of the same
group of organs. Now
you can see where the **hymen** is, at the entrance to the vagina,
and you can follow the passage which runs from the ovarian
tube down through the womb, cervix and vagina into the vulva.

At some time during puberty you will begin to release a fertile ovum from one or other of your ovaries, usually alternately, every four weeks or so. This process is called **ovulation**. At ovulation, the new ovum is caught by the fimbriae when it is released from the ovary and is then propelled down the ovarian tube into the womb. The journey usually takes about three days, but the ovum is only fertile for two days or so, after which it dies.

The inside of the womb has a special lining (made of very fine tissue and called the **endometrium**) which is grown each time a woman ovulates, just in case it is needed. Of course, usually it is *not* needed because the ovum is not going to develop into a baby, and the lining is then shed (cast off). When this happens, the tissue of the lining, together with the dead ovum and a small amount of blood, passes out of the womb through the cervix. For perhaps four or five days the blood and tissue (called the **menses**) flow down through the vagina and out of the vulva little by little. This is the process I mentioned on page 16 called menstruation, or having a **period**.

After a few days a new endometrium begins to grow in the womb, a new ovum is released, and the whole process is repeated: this is called the **menstrual cycle** (a cycle is something which happens again and again). If the ovum is fertilised, however, the endometrium is not shed: the ovum, now beginning to grow, settles in it and becomes attached to it.

As the baby-to-be grows the womb grows too, expanding so that it can hold the baby safely. At the time of birth the cervix and vagina and vulva—together called the **birth canal**—all stretch to many times their normal size so that the baby can pass through easily on its way to the outside world. While the baby is growing in the womb there is no ovulation and no menstruation: they do not start again until a few weeks or months after the birth. Pregnancy and birth are described on page 56-66.

Because menstrual blood and urine are both discharged through the vulva, some women believe that the vulva must be a 'dirty' organ. However, both the blood and urine are perfectly clean, and so is the vulva.

Menstruation can cause some inconvenience and discomfort, and may take some time to get used to. After the first few months, however, girls accept it as a natural process. It is certainly an important part of every woman's life, taking place 12 or 13 times each year for perhaps 30 to 35 years, when it finally stops. There is much more information about it on pages 85-87.

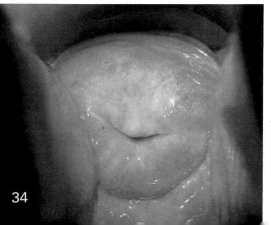

Here is an ovum seen from inside ovarian tube. The ovum is little n than one-tenth of one millimet diameter (about the size of a pinhe here it is enlarged about 250 ti

This is the cervix seen from the vagina. It is about two centimetres wide, so this picture is about three times larger than life-size. The opening itself is much smaller, but it will expand to a diameter of about 10 centimetres when a baby is being born.

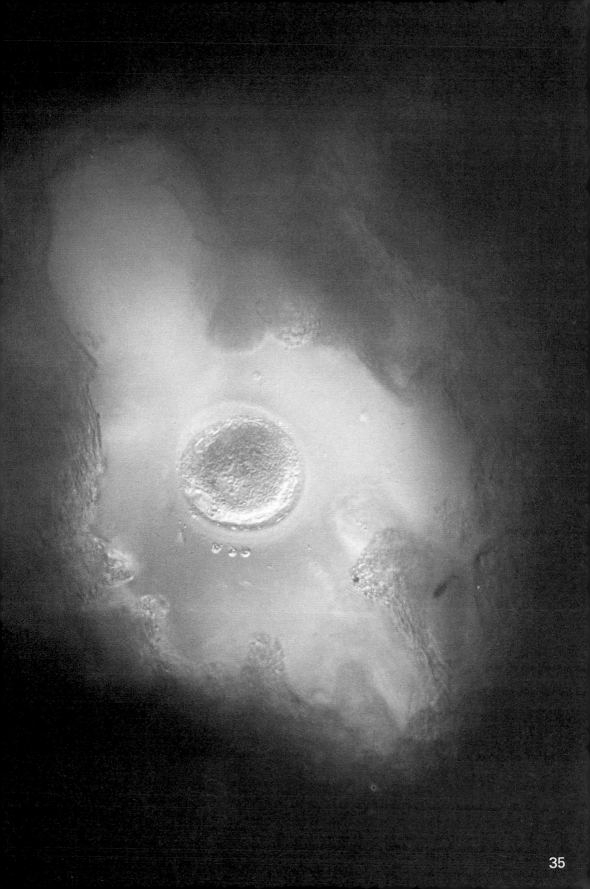

boy to man

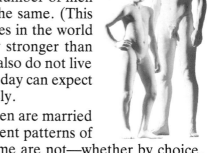

For every 100 girls born in Britain, 105 boys are born—but more boys than girls die early, so the number of men and women reaching adulthood is about the same. (This is true also of the balance between the sexes in the world as a whole.) Men are generally physically stronger than women, yet are more likely to fall ill. Men also do not live as long as women: boys and girls aged 10 today can expect to live to about 75 and 80 years respectively.

About the same proportion of men as women are married (not exactly the same because of the different patterns of divorce and remarriage) and about the same are not—whether by choice, lack of opportunity or misfortune. Many unmarried men are fathers and many married men are not.

The role of the male in reproduction is much less demanding than that of the female. He has only to produce the sperm which will fertilise the ovum and to make sure that it reaches the ovum (we shall find out later how this is done), and his physical contribution is finished. The female's role, on the other hand, only starts with producing the ovum and receiving the sperm. Thereafter she must carry the developing baby inside her body, nourishing and protecting it for nine months before birth, and breast-feeding it for a few months after it is born.

Of course, the social role of fatherhood involves much more than simply producing sperms, just as the social role of motherhood extends far beyond bearing and nursing the baby. Father and mother usually both share the many responsibilities of bringing up a family. However, it is easy to see what a big difference in the lives of men and women is created by the inequality between their reproductive roles. While many women welcome or accept the motherhood role allotted to them by nature, it is easy, too, to appreciate why many others resent the much greater freedom of the male, and feel that their child-bearing role puts them at a disadvantage.

Nature certainly seems to be extravagant with the male. At most, a woman bears only a few babies in her life, whereas a man produces several *billion* sperms in his lifetime—more than enough to populate the whole world!

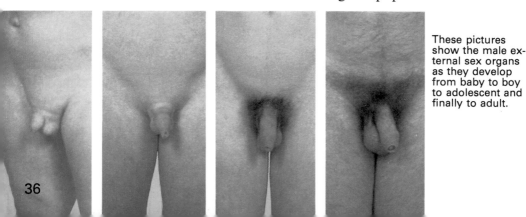

These pictures show the male external sex organs as they develop from baby to boy to adolescent and finally to adult.

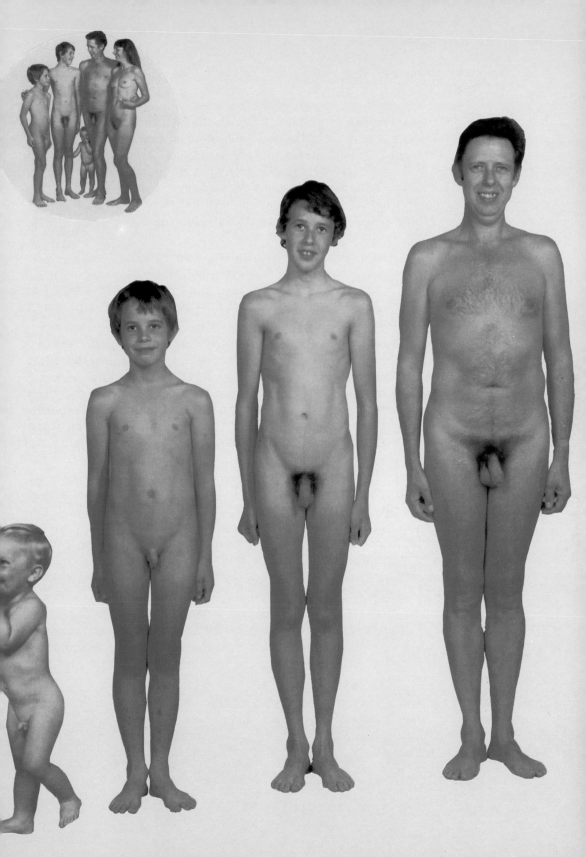

The sperms which are the male's contribution to reproduction are made by the testicles, which also make the sex hormones which control a man's sexual development. The temperature in the scrotum is about 2° centigrade lower than the temperature inside the body. We know that the testicles make sperms best at this lower temperature, but not *why* this should be. It does seem strange that such vital glands should be in such an exposed and unprotected position! However, this is why the scrotum contracts, drawing the testicles up to the warmer crotch, when it is exposed to the cold.

The testicles start to enlarge at the beginning of puberty (around 11½ on average) but do not usually begin to produce sperms until two years or so later. They will then produce many millions of sperms each day—several hundred each minute!—and will carry on doing so all through the man's adult life. (The medical names for sperms and testicles are **spermatozoa** and **testes**.)

The other male external sex organ is the penis. This varies greatly in shape and size from one man to another. At birth the end of the penis, called the **glans**, is covered by a sleeve of skin called the **foreskin** or **prepuce**. At first, the foreskin is actually attached to the glans, but after a time (which may be anything from a few months to several years) it becomes loose and can move freely over the glans. The glans is very sensitive, and the foreskin helps to protect it from harm.

However, in some places and religions it is the custom to cut the foreskin off. This is called **circumcision**, and is usually done shortly after birth or during childhood. In some boys the foreskin is too tight for comfort, and has to be removed for this reason, but there is seldom any other medical reason for circumcision. Whether a man is circumcised or uncircumcised has no effect on his sexual performance.

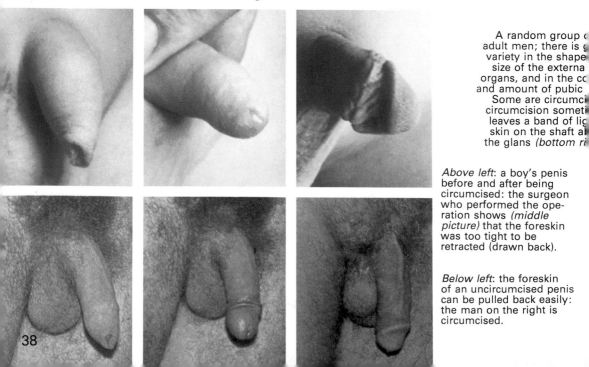

A random group o
adult men; there is g
variety in the shape
size of the externa
organs, and in the cc
and amount of pubic
Some are circumci
circumcision someti
leaves a band of lig
skin on the shaft a
the glans *(bottom ri*

Above left: a boy's penis before and after being circumcised: the surgeon who performed the operation shows *(middle picture)* that the foreskin was too tight to be retracted (drawn back).

Below left: the foreskin of an uncircumcised penis can be pulled back easily: the man on the right is circumcised.

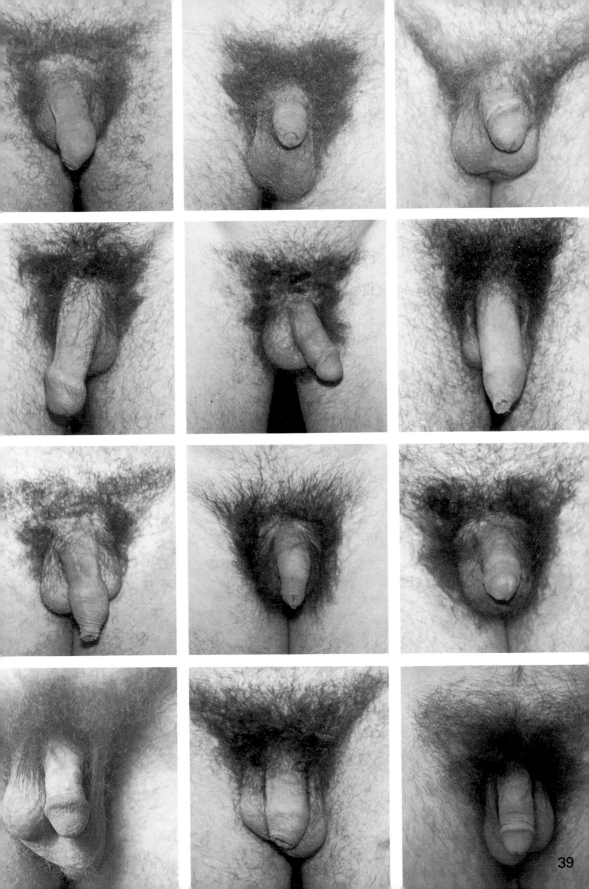

39

The testicles are often of different sizes, and one probably hangs lower than the other (usually the left one). The testicles normally descend into the scrotum from inside the groin shortly before birth; sometimes, however, one or both may still be inside the groin at birth. These are described as **undescended**. They nearly always descend naturally, but sometimes one or both may have to be helped down into the scrotum by a simple operation, as you can see below.

If a man loses one of his testicles, perhaps because of an accident or a disease, the other will continue to work and his fertility will not be affected. If he loses both testicles, however, he will of course no longer be able to produce sperms or sex hormones, and will therefore be **infertile** or **sterile** and will lose some of his sexual character. (The same things apply to a woman who loses one or both of her ovaries.) Removing both testicles is called **castration** and a man who has been castrated is called a **eunuch**.

There are three more points to mention before we look at the internal organs. First, there is great variety in the amount, colour, type and distribution of male hair. Some men have a great deal of body hair and some very little; some have coarse hair and some soft; some go bald and some do not. You may hear it said that these things indicate **virility** (that is, sexual **potency** and ability) or the lack of it, but the simple fact is that they have no significance at all: hair is just hair.

Secondly, a word about **acne**, which affects boys and girls, but boys more than girls. Acne is not a disease, it is not something you catch from someone else, and it is not caused by any sort of sexual activity or bad hygiene. Some of the hormones which start to work at puberty cause changes in the skin; these hormones are often over-active for a time, resulting in the outbreak of pimples on the face, neck, back and shoulders which is called acne.

It is easy to infect these pimples and make them worse, so you must not squeeze or 'pop' them. Regular washing with soap and water helps. If the acne gets bad, chemists sell creams or lotions which may help; if it gets very bad, you may have to see a doctor. However unsightly it may be for a time, you can take comfort from the fact that acne will go away in the end.

Finally, boys sometimes worry about the small white spots which may appear on the shaft of the penis at puberty; these are normal and need no treatment.

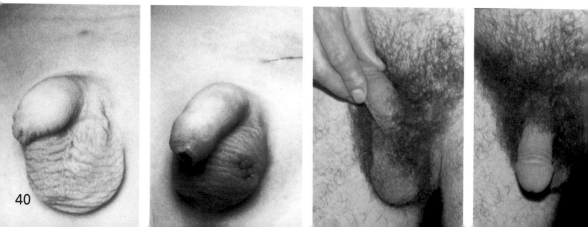

Here are two cases of acne, one much worse than the other. These acne pictures are included in this 'boy to man' chapter because acne is most common among boys. However, many girls also suffer from it, and for the same reasons.

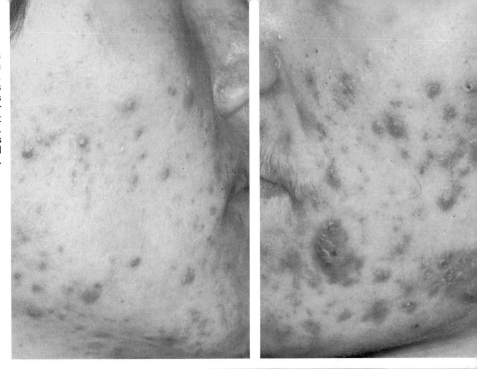

Freckles are quite common, usually on the face, arms and upper body. They are caused by uneven distribution of melanin (the pigment which makes skin brown), and are often found in people with red hair.

Bottom right: male nipples are leftovers from the fact that both sexes grow from the same cells in the embryo (explained later on in the book). Men's nipples can be small or large, and their chests can be hairy or smooth: one is no more virile than the other. Many people have a small 'third nipple', as you can see *(far right)*.

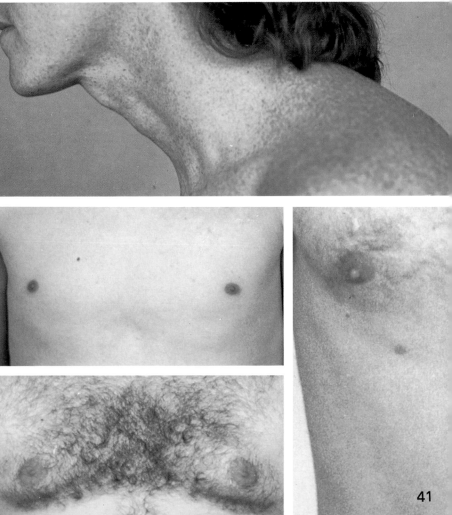

boy *(far left)* had an undescended testicle; *(middle picture)* testicle has been moved from the groin down into the scrotum by a surgeon. The two small scars quickly heal and disappear.

The loss of a single testicle is common; it does no harm and, as you see *(nearest picture)*, is not even noticeable.

The male internal sex organs are the **seminal vesicles** and **prostate gland**. At about the same time as the testicles start producing sperms, these glands begin to produce a liquid called **seminal fluid**. Two tubes (sometimes called **sperm tubes**) connect the testicles to the seminal vesicles, and these in turn are connected to the prostate gland.

When the sexual system is stimulated, the sperms are propelled from the testicles up these tubes to be stored in the seminal vesicles, and mix with the seminal fluid there. The resulting mixture of fluid and sperms has its own name: **semen**. This is the white liquid mentioned on page 16 which is ejaculated from the penis. The seminal fluid is necessary to carry the sperms because they are so small: in fact semen is composed of about 100 parts of seminal fluid to 1 part of sperms, and one drop of semen contains *millions* of sperms. The seminal fluid also nourishes the sperms and gives them the ability to move under their own power.

The urethra passes through the prostate gland, where it is joined by tubes from the seminal vesicles. From this point, therefore, the penis becomes the outlet not only for urine but also for semen. (The bladder, incidentally, is *not* a sex organ, and the urethra is part of the sexual system only in males, not in females.)

Because semen is discharged through the same tube as urine, some people say it is 'dirty' or harmful. This is not true: it is as natural and healthy a product of the body as blood, sweat or mother's milk.

Now please take a few minutes to study the pictures numbered 1 to 5 below and on the next three pages. These are arranged in exactly the same way as those showing the female internal sex organs (pages 30-33).

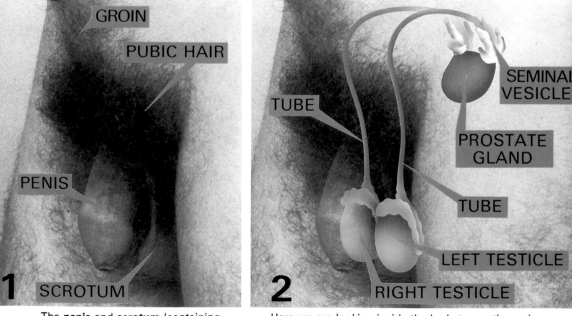

1 GROIN / PUBIC HAIR / PENIS / SCROTUM

2 TUBE / SEMINAL VESICLE / PROSTATE GLAND / TUBE / LEFT TESTICLE / RIGHT TESTICLE

The **penis** and **scrotum** (containing the testicles) are the *external* sex organs. In an adult man they are partly hidden by thick **pubic hair**.

Here we are looking inside the body to see the main *internal* sex organs. The **testicles**, inside the scrotum, hang side-by-side behind the penis and are connected by tubes to the **seminal vesicles** and **prostate gland** inside.

The pictures on these and the next two pages are arranged exactly like those of the woman on pages 30–33: the full-page pictures are enlargements of the areas outlined in black on the small full-length insets. Three views are shown (three-quarter on this page, front and side overleaf) so that, if you turn this page to and fro, you will be able to get a three-dimensional view of all the organs. Each picture in the sequence adds more information.

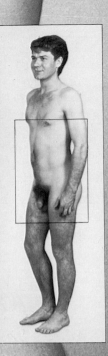

NAVEL

TUBES carrying urine from kidneys to bladder

BLADDER storing urine

junction (inside prostate) where tubes from testicles meet tube from bladder

URETHRA carrying urine from bladder

complete the picture, the **bladder** and **urethra** are added. The bladder is *not* ex organ, but the seminal vesicles and prostate gland are all attached to it.

SPINE

PELVIS

In the picture below, some of the bones are shown: the pelvis, the pubic bone, the start of the two thigh-bones and the spine. (You can feel the pubic bone, the outer edges of the pelvis and, of course, the spine quite easily through your flesh.) The empty space around and above the bladder is filled with the intestines (not shown), which end in the bowel and anus, shown on page 45.

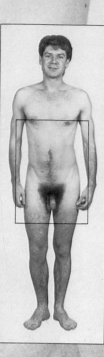

BLADDER

TUBE
from testicle to
seminal vesicles

PUBIC BONE
lying in front
of bladder and
prostate gland

TESTICLE

URETHRA

SCROTUM
containing
testicles

PENIS
enclosing
urethra

4

Here on these two pages are the front and side views of the same group of organs as on page 43.

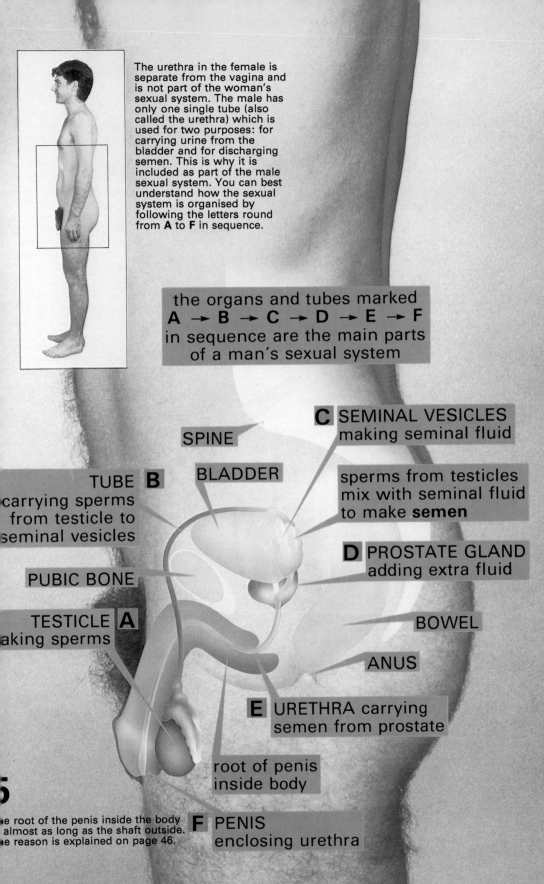

The urethra in the female is separate from the vagina and is not part of the woman's sexual system. The male has only one single tube (also called the urethra) which is used for two purposes: for carrying urine from the bladder and for discharging semen. This is why it is included as part of the male sexual system. You can best understand how the sexual system is organised by following the letters round from **A** to **F** in sequence.

the organs and tubes marked
A → **B** → **C** → **D** → **E** → **F**
in sequence are the main parts
of a man's sexual system

C SEMINAL VESICLES
making seminal fluid

SPINE

BLADDER

sperms from testicles
mix with seminal fluid
to make **semen**

TUBE **B**
carrying sperms
from testicle to
seminal vesicles

D PROSTATE GLAND
adding extra fluid

PUBIC BONE

TESTICLE **A**
aking sperms

BOWEL

ANUS

E URETHRA carrying
semen from prostate

root of penis
inside body

e root of the penis inside the body
almost as long as the shaft outside.
e reason is explained on page 46.

F PENIS
enclosing urethra

During puberty, as the external sex organs grow larger, the penis increases its ability to become long and hard when it is stimulated, and this is called having an **erection**.

Semen is ejaculated when the penis is erect. Although ejaculation only begins during puberty, erections usually start very early—indeed, many baby boys have an erection just after they are born (although this has no special meaning), and almost all young boys have them from time to time.

The tissue inside the penis is full of blood-vessels which can stretch and swell up and become hard when extra blood is pumped into them. This is what happens when a man has an erection. It is because the root of the penis is held several centimetres inside the body (as shown in the picture on page 45) that the erect penis is strong enough to stand out from the body.

The size and shape of the erect penis varies a lot from one man to another. It may bend to the left or right, or up or down, or rise higher or lower than another. A smaller penis usually swells up more than a larger one, so both will be about the same size when erect (on average about 15 or 16 centimetres long). Some will stay hard for a longer or shorter time than others.

Some men think that the penis is the symbol of a man's virility, and that its size—particularly when erect—must therefore be very important indeed. However, except in rare cases, neither size nor shape makes any practical difference to sexual potency or performance.

When the penis is erect, the opening from the bladder into the urethra is squeezed shut; when the penis is relaxed, however, the openings from the seminal vesicles and prostate gland into the urethra close and the tube from the bladder opens. It is therefore difficult for a man to urinate when he has an erection, or for semen to become mixed with urine when he ejaculates.

At puberty erections begin to happen much more frequently than during boyhood and often, but not always, will be followed by an ejaculation of semen. This may happen at any time or place, even when you are asleep, and sometimes at awkward moments. You may get erections several times a day or only very occasionally: the frequency varies enormously, and has no particular significance. Erections are often accompanied by powerful **erotic** (that is, sexually exciting) thoughts, or are caused by such thoughts.

The sequence of pictures on the right shows the process of erection; the foreskin retracts as the penis becomes erect.

Facing, above:
You can see from these eight random examples how much variation there is in the male erection. The size of the penis when relaxed gives no indication of its size when erect (compare the examples on the top left and the bottom right).

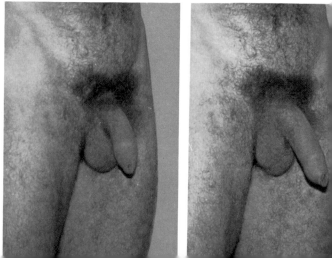

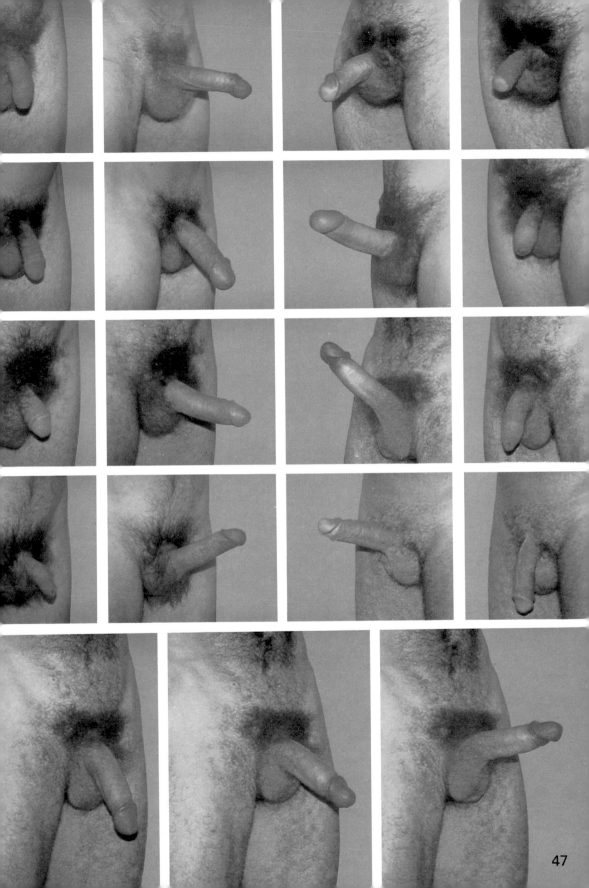

47

male and female

We have now looked in detail at the sexual systems of the female and the male, and there are some interesting points of comparison. You have probably already noticed, from the pictures and descriptions, the similarity between the ovaries and the testicles.

There is a name for both of these together: the **gonads**. In other words, the gonads are the glands which produce the gametes (ova and sperms) and the sex hormones.

Although the ovaries and testicles are glands which have the same role in female and male, we have seen that they perform their jobs in completely different ways. The ovaries together release only a few hundred ova during 30-35 years, while the testicles each produce many millions of sperms every day through the whole of a man's life.

The vagina and the penis also have similar functions, as we shall see in the next section. The clitoris, too, has similarities with the penis. Both become very sensitive when erect, and give pleasurable feelings: these are in fact the principal organs of sexual pleasure.

The pictures below are the same as those of the man on page 45 (now facing the other way) and the woman on page 33. Here only the sexual parts are named.

In the man, follow the journey of the sperms produced in the testicles **A** through the tubes **B** to be stored in the seminal vesicles **C**. Here the sperms mix with the seminal fluid produced by the vesicles. When the man ejaculates, this seminal fluid is propelled through the prostate gland **D**, where it mixes with extra fluid produced by this gland, then out through the urethra **E** and penis **F**.

In the woman, follow the journey of an ovum released from one of the ovaries **A** into one of the ovarian tubes **B** and down through these into the womb **C**. If it is not fertilised, the ovum will be discharged at menstruation through the vagina **D**; if it is fertilised, it will grow in the womb into a baby, which will be born through the vagina.

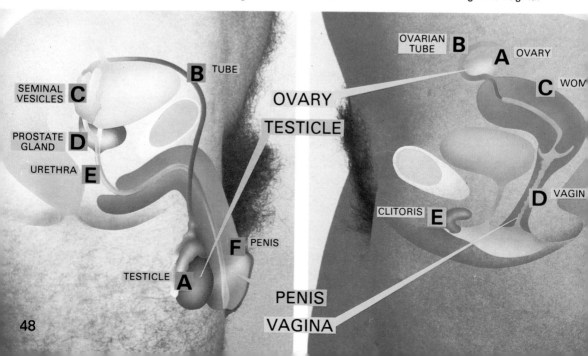

reproduction

Reproduction is the making of babies: in other words, the process by which one generation creates the next generation, by which parents have children.

We already know (page 15) that for this to happen the mother's ovum must first be united with one of the father's sperms when both are fertile. This is the essential first step of reproduction. It is important to be quite clear about this: *there is no other way for a baby to be created*.

We know, too (page 34) that an ovum remains fertile only for two days or so as it travels down the ovarian tube; and (page 42) that when sperms leave the testicles they are stored in the seminal vesicles. Finally, we know (page 42) that sperms can move by themselves and (page 46) that they are ejaculated in semen through the penis when it is erect. We can now bring all this knowledge together and find out *why* these things are as they are.

To give the fertile ovum in the ovarian tube the best chance to be united with a sperm, the man's semen must be discharged as close as possible to it. This happens when a woman and a man join together in an act which is called **coitus**. It is also called **sexual intercourse** or just **intercourse**, or **copulation**, or the **sex act**, or simply **making love** or **having sex**, or just **sex**.

The sperms—produced by the testicles at the rate of several hundred every minute—have been propelled up the sperm tubes and into the seminal vesicles where they are stored.

1 A fertile ovum, moving down one of the ovarian tubes towards the womb, cannot be fertilised until it is united with one of the many millions of sperms waiting in the seminal vesicles of the male. So the sperm has to reach the ovum. How can it do this?

It is the time of month when a fertile ovum has just been released from an ovary. It has been captured by the fimbriae and drawn into the ovarian tube on its way to the womb.

coitus

In coitus the man puts his erect penis into the woman's vagina, through the vulva, and ejaculates so that his semen is discharged near the cervix.

Before coitus can take place, the man and the woman must become ready for it. As soon as they begin to touch and hold each other closely, and perhaps kiss and stroke each other, several changes begin to take place in their sex organs.

In the man, the penis becomes erect and hard enough for him to be able to push it into the vagina: this is the purpose of the male erection. In the woman, the clitoris and nipples also become erect, and the vagina relaxes and widens, producing a special liquid which lubricates it so that the penis will be able to enter it easily. The testicles and the vulva also swell up, the scrotum tightens, and the vagina and the glans of the penis and clitoris all become very sensitive (as does the skin over much of the body).

These changes help to make coitus more comfortable and enjoyable for each partner. When both are ready, and the penis enters and moves inside the vagina, they will feel increasing pleasure and excitement.

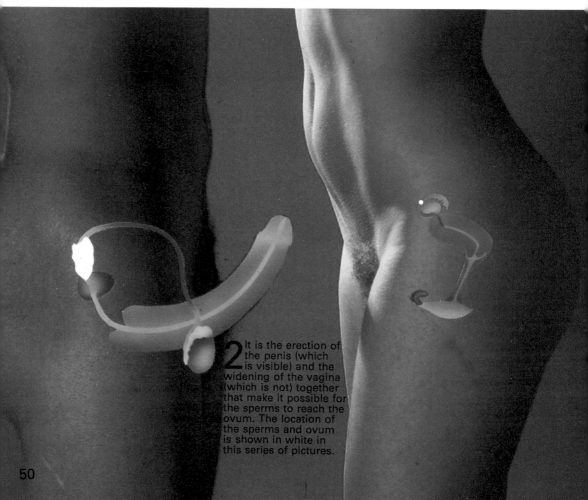

2 It is the erection of the penis (which is visible) and the widening of the vagina (which is not) together that make it possible for the sperms to reach the ovum. The location of the sperms and ovum is shown in white in this series of pictures.

3 When the vagina is relaxed, stretched and lubricated, the penis can enter it comfortably. The sperms are still in the seminal vesicles. Usually a couple lie down for coitus, but it can also take place with them standing up.

conception

The climax of pleasure and satisfaction in coitus, when the muscles tighten and then relax, is called **orgasm**. For the man, this is also the moment when he ejaculates. As far as the requirements of reproduction are concerned, it is not necessary for the woman to have an orgasm: whether she does or not has no effect on the ability of the sperms to reach the ovum. After the man ejaculates, his penis soon begins to relax and he withdraws it, leaving the semen in the vagina. Both partners will probably feel sleepy afterwards.

Because the erect penis fills the vagina, the semen is ejaculated very near the cervix. Because the sperms are made active by the semen which has carried them this far, a great many of them can now find their way through the cervix into the womb. Some will already be travelling through the cervix within a minute or two of ejaculation. An hour or two later the strongest and fastest of the sperms, swimming on to the top end of the womb and into one of the ovarian tubes, may meet an ovum (but only if the coitus is taking place shortly after ovulation).

These are the bare facts of coitus. So far I have only described its role in reproduction, which is purely physical, but there is a great deal more to making love than just the physical union. The mind and heart are also involved: both partners have emotions which are aroused before, during and after coitus, and these are very important. (There is more about this on pages 71-72, 81-84 and 105.)

Although the semen of each ejaculation contains many millions of sperms, only one needs to unite with an ovum to fertilise it. If this happens, the sperm and ovum join together in the moment of **conception**, and a new life is beginning. When conception takes place we say that the woman **conceives** and that the baby is conceived.

4 This is the moment of orgasm: the sperms, mixed with the seminal fluid, are propelled along the urethra and ejaculated into the end of the vagina near the cervix.

Sperms swim up through the cervix like a shoal of fishes. A single ejaculation contains hundreds of millions of sperms but most will not even reach here. Each has a big head and a long tail which moves like a snake. They are so small that it takes a powerful microscope to see them like this.

5 Within minutes of ejaculation, many of the sperms nearest to the cervix have left the seminal fluid and are already travelling through the cervix and on into the womb. Meantime the man has withdrawn his penis from the vagina and both relax. The coitus is over.

You can see how very small the sperms are compared with the ovum: in fact the ovum is thousands of times larger— yet one for each person in the world would fit inside a hen's egg. There are several sperms trying to enter this one, but only one will be successful.

6 An hour or two later thousands of the most energetic sperms have got to the ovarian tubes and some have met up with the waiting ovum.
Fertilisation and conception are about to take place.
The man's part in the process of reproduction has finished with his ejaculation, but the woman's part is only just beginning.

I have already said (page 49) that the *only* way that conception can take place is when an ovum is fertilised by a sperm. Now I must add that the **only natural way** and time and place for conception is by coitus during the two days or so in the menstrual cycle when the ovum has left the ovary and is in the ovarian tube before it dies. (I say the only *natural* way because it is possible nowadays to bring fertile ova and sperms together by artificial means; however, this can only be done in very special circumstances.)

Conception is the time at which the whole life of the new human being is shaped: not only its gender but its whole **inheritance**.

The inheritance is contained within the ovum and sperm in invisibly small structures which are instruction-carriers. The instructions are called **genes** and the carriers **chromosomes**. There are 46 of these, arranged in 23 pairs, in each and every one of the billions of cells in our bodies (except the gametes: the ova and sperms).

One chromosome in each pair comes from our mother and the other from our father; in some of the pairs the maternal genes dominate, in others the paternal genes. Together the 23 pairs carry all the genes which give each human being her or his unique pattern of physical and mental qualities and characteristics: the frame, the colour of hair, eyes and skin, features, intelligence, physical strengths, weaknesses and so on.

The gametes are special: they contain 23 chromosomes only, one from each of the 23 pairs. When they unite at conception, the 23 chromosomes in the sperm combine with the 23 in the ovum, creating another unique code of 46. This is the baby's inheritance from its parents. The transmission of genes through the gametes from parents to offspring, from one generation to the next, is called **heredity**.

The gender of the baby-to-be is fixed by one of the chromosome pairs called the **sex chromosomes**. Females have two the same which are known as XX; males have two different ones known as X and Y. Therefore all ova carry an X chromosome (because either half of XX is X) but sperms are of two types: X and Y. Each testicle makes both types in approximately equal numbers.

If the sperm which fertilises the ovum is type X, the new baby will be XX and therefore female; if the sperm is type Y, the new baby will be XY, and therefore male. So the sex of a baby is fixed by the sperm, but of course the father himself has no say in the choice: it is pure chance whether an X-type or a Y-type sperm reaches the ovum first.

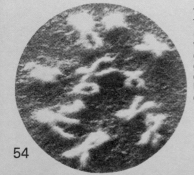

These are chromosomes. There are about fifty trillion (50,000,000,000,000) cells in the adult body (about 5000 cells together are the size of a grain of sand) and each cell contains 46 chromosomes. Each chromosome in turn contains hundreds of genes....

Three generations of one fam father, son and grandson—illus the close resemblance four many, but by no means all, fam The grandfather is 78, his son and his grandson is 5 years The inset portraits show all t generations at the same

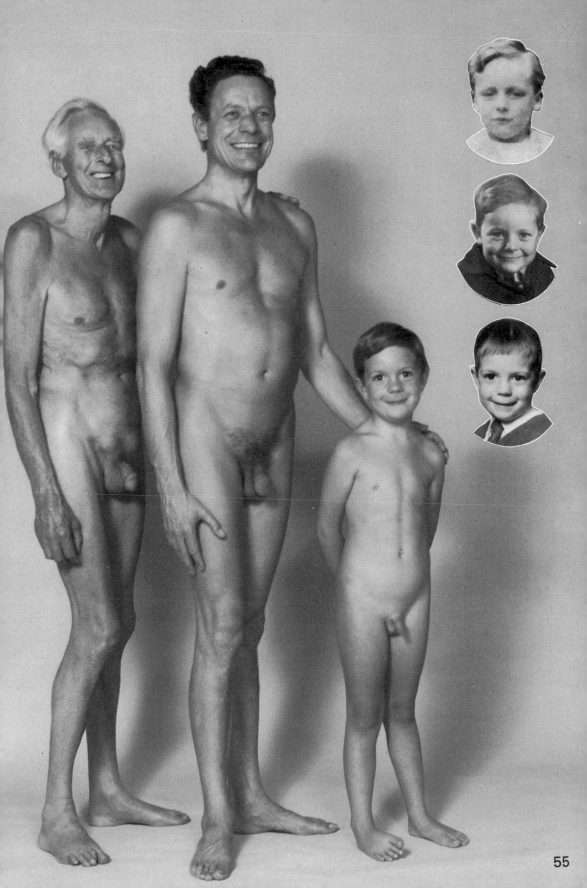

pregnancy

How does a single fertilised cell become a baby? Strange as it may seem, the whole complicated programme of development is already contained in the fertilised ovum, although this is no bigger than a pinhead. It 'knows' exactly what to do, and how and when to do it.

The ovum grows first by dividing, shown in the photographs below. The cells not only multiply very rapidly; after a time they also begin to separate into the many different types of cells (over 200) which will eventually form such varied parts of the body as bones, flesh, eyes, brain, nerves, and so on. In fact within three months all the parts will have been formed in miniature; for the rest of the pregnancy they have only to grow larger.

As the ball of cells grows it travels down the ovarian tube into the womb. Here, about a week after fertilisation, it fixes itself to the endometrium (the lining) which has grown specially to receive it. It is now called an **embryo**. As the endometrium is now needed to protect and feed the growing embryo, it does not die; there will be no more menstruation until after the birth.

This means that the mother-to-be misses a period about two weeks after conception, and this will be the first sign to her that she may be pregnant. (It is quite normal to miss a period without being pregnant: for example, an illness or worry can often cause a woman to miss a period, and sometimes there seems to be no reason at all.) It is not until after the third missed period that a doctor will be able to confirm the pregnancy by examination, although there are chemical tests which can be used earlier if necessary.

It is usual for doctors and mothers to consider pregnancy as starting on the first day of the last menstrual cycle. On this basis, the average pregnancy lasts about 40 weeks (in other words, nine calendar months plus one week). In this book, however, we are calculating from the time of conception in order to show the correct age on each picture, so the pregnancy illustrated on the following pages lasts 38 weeks (nine months *less* one week).

One of the sperms has penetrated into the ovum, leaving its tail outside. The 23 chromosomes in the head of the sperm line up with the 23 in the ovum and join together. This is the moment of fertilisation.

The fertilised ovum contains the complete set of instructions for creating a unique new human being. About a day after fertilisation the process of growth begins when the single cell divides into two.

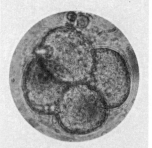

The second division, when the two cells become four, happens about 20 hours after the first; and the third, when four become eight, about ten hours later. Each cell has its own individual development programme.

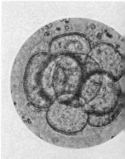

Four more divisions will turn these eight cells into 128 by the end of the week after fertilisation; this time the growing of cells will have travelled down the ovarian tube and settled in the womb

56

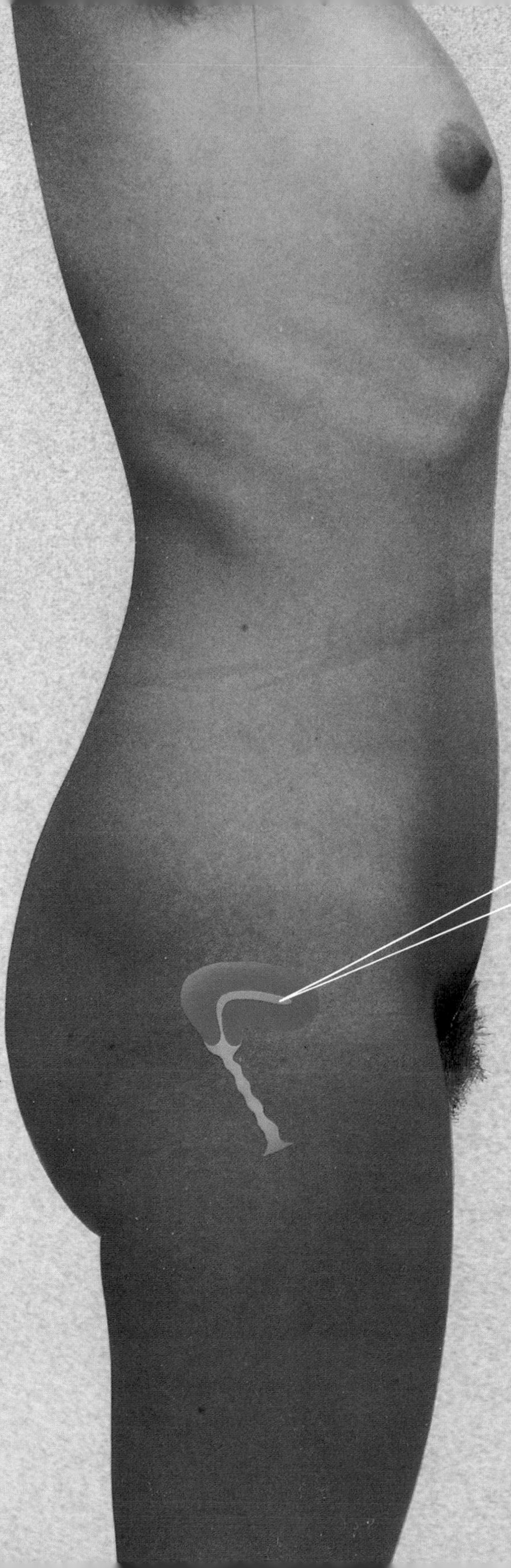

1 At the end of month 1—
the end of week 4—
the embryo is 4 or 5
millimetres long. It is shown
life-size above and ten times
larger than life in the photograph below. The head
and neck are about half
the overall length; the
eyes, mouth, heart and
spine are just beginning
to appear, but the embryo
still has a tail and is not
yet distinctively human.

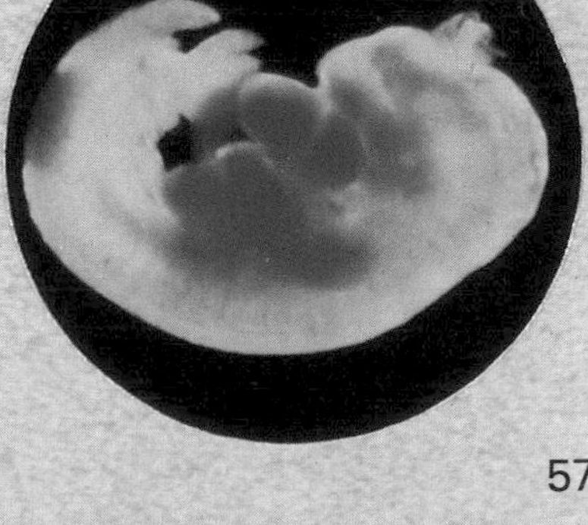

On these two pages you can see the growing baby-to-be at the end of each of its first four months of growth:

  month 1: *above*
  month 2: *below*
  month 3: *right*
  month 4: *facing page*

In these three months it grows from 4 or 5 to 150 millimetres, and from only a gram or two to 250 grams. **All the pictures are life-size.**

A pregnancy is measured in months or in weeks—both are shown here. The weight of an average fetus at the end of each month is given in grams: there are about 30 grams to an ounce, and 250 grams are about half-a-pound. The average length is given in millimetres: there are 25 to an inch. The length is measured not from head to foot but from head to rump (bottom) because the fetus is always curled up.

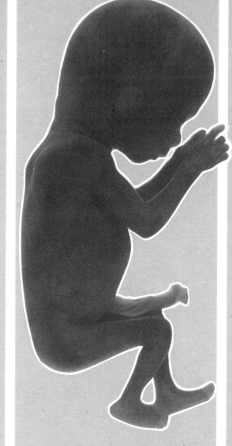

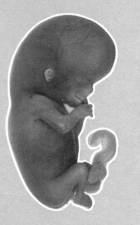

At 9 weeks you can already see the head, arms and legs quite clearly. From now on the baby-to-be is no longer an embryo. It is now called a **fetus**.

At 13 weeks the fetus (here shown actual size) is growing very quickly: with six months still to go before birth, eyes and mouth, hands and feet are already perfectly formed.

In the three pictures at the bottom of this page, our mother-to-be is progressing through months 2, 3 and 4 of her pregnancy. Her belly will not begin to swell visibly until the fourth month—inside, however, the womb is expanding and the baby is growing and developing fast all the time.

At 17 weeks *(right)* the is beginning to fill our p Here you can see the **place** the **umbilical cord** and **amniotic sac** which a explained on pag

2 end of month 2
weight only a few grams
length about 50 millimetres

3 end of month 3
weight about 70 grams
length about 100 millimetres

4 end of month 4
weight about 250 grams
length about 150 millimetr

week 13

week 17

PLACENTA

UMBILICAL CORD

AMNIOTIC SAC

We are now in month 5, about half-way through the pregnancy—which is now clearly visible in the bulging shape of the mother's belly. The growing fetus is fully formed and is already moving about in the womb, kicking and even sucking its thumb, as you can see in the picture below. It also sleeps from time to time, but not at the same time as the mother does.

The fetus grows inside the **amniotic sac**, a bag of membrane filled with liquid, which acts like a soft cushion to protect the fetus which floats inside. It is joined to the womb by a thick cord called the **umbilical cord**. Where this cord meets the lining of the womb it widens to make a kind of root called the **placenta** which holds the fetus tight to the side of the womb.

The fetus cannot breathe or eat until it is born, but inside the womb it receives the oxygen (the life-giving gas in air) and the food it needs from its mother through the umbilical cord. It also produces waste, and this is passed out of its body not through the urethra and bowel but back through the umbilical cord.

The mother-to-be has to take great care of herself to make sure that the fetus she is carrying is well-nourished and in good health. She must watch her diet, take plenty of exercise and avoid anything which may be harmful to the fetus (such as cigarettes and alcohol and unnecessary drugs). She may feel cravings for unusual foods, perhaps pickled gherkins or potato crisps—almost anything, maybe even coal or toothpaste or soap—but these cravings disappear after a time.

The mother's own body is changing to accommodate the growing fetus, and her weight is increasing more than the weight of the fetus. The womb, placenta and amniotic sac are all growing with the fetus, and so of course is the amount of liquid in the amniotic sac. The enlarging womb is now beginning to squeeze the other internal organs out of their usual positions; this becomes increasingly uncomfortable for the mother as the pregnancy continues through the later months.

By the end of the fifth month the fetus has become bigger than this page. This picture shows its face and hands life-size. Its fingernails and eye lashes are beginning to grow and it can open its eyelids. It sucks its thumb and can clench its fists. It is quite energetic and its mother can often feel it moving about in the womb.

5 This is the end of month 5—the end of week 21—and the baby now weighs just over half a kilo. It is about 200 millimetres long from crown to rump; if it could stand it would be about 300mm tall. The mother is gaining half a kilo in weight each week.

By the sixth month the fetus begins to have a chance of surviving if for any reason it is born prematurely (before the due time); its chances improve with every extra week of growth in the womb.

The fetus can turn easily from side to side within its amniotic sac but not so easily head over heels. Usually, however, some time during the seventh or eighth month it settles head down (that is, with the head towards the cervix), as you can see below. This is the easiest and most usual position for the birth. Sometimes, however, the fetus does not turn and stays head up. This is called the **breech position** (breech is another word for buttocks) and a birth with the baby in this position is called a **breech birth**.

If the womb seems to be growing more quickly than normal, this may be because there is not just one fetus in the womb but two. On average there is one pair of **twins** in every hundred babies born (triplets are much rarer, and quadruplets rarer still—perhaps one set in every half-million births).

Usually twins happen because the mother produces two ova instead of one, and each is fertilised by a different sperm. It is then an equal chance whether each baby will be male or female, so the mother may give birth to two boys or two girls or a girl and a boy, and they will be no more alike than ordinary brothers and sisters. These are called **fraternal twins**.

It is also possible, however, for a single fertilised ovum to divides into two cells which then begin to grow separately. This produces **identical twins**: that is, two girls or two boys who (because they come from the same ovum and sperm) are very much alike in every way.

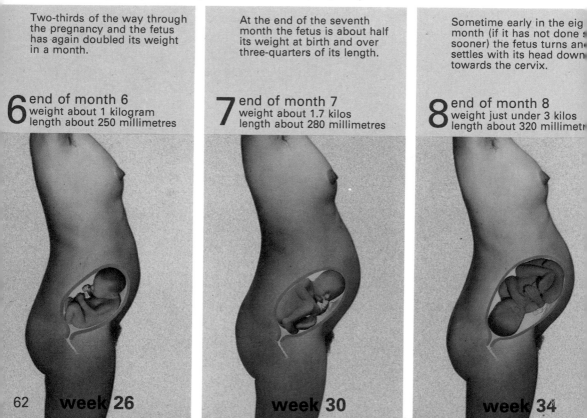

Two-thirds of the way through the pregnancy and the fetus has again doubled its weight in a month.

6 end of month 6
weight about 1 kilogram
length about 250 millimetres

At the end of the seventh month the fetus is about half its weight at birth and over three-quarters of its length.

7 end of month 7
weight about 1.7 kilos
length about 280 millimetres

Sometime early in the eig month (if it has not done sooner) the fetus turns an settles with its head down towards the cervix.

8 end of month 8
weight just under 3 kilos
length about 320 millimetr

week 26

week 30

week 34

9 Finally the baby is ready to be born, about 38 weeks after conception, although it may arrive a little earlier or a little later. It now weighs about 3.5 kilos and its length is about 320 millimetres (about 500 full length). The mother probably now weighs about 12 kilos more than her normal weight.

birth

At last the baby is ready to be born. After all these months, the whole birth itself will take only a few hours, and the final stages only a few minutes.

The mother knows when the birth is about to start because she feels strong **contractions** (sudden tightening of the muscles) in the walls of the womb at intervals of about three minutes. This is the beginning of **labour**. Little by little, the contractions stretch open the birth canal: the cervix, the vagina and the vulva.

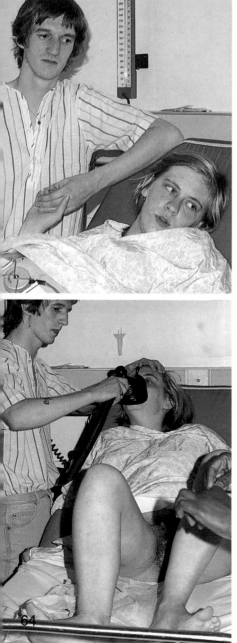

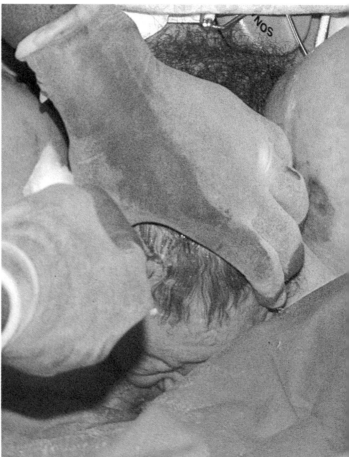

2 a.m. on a Saturday morning in August in North London: Donna, who has already begun labour, arrives at the hospital with her husband Gary.

She makes herself comfortable in bed and a monitor to check the baby's heartbeats is strapped to her belly.

2.30: the contractions are growing stronger and Gary helps by giving his wife anesthetic gas through the tube and mouthpiece.

2.45: (above) the baby's head begins to emerge; the midwife (wearing rubber gloves) steadies the head.

A few seconds later: (above right) It's a boy! The rest of the body emerges very quickly, held gently by the midwife with a finger under each armpit. Note the umbilical cord and the thin coating of wax (called vernix) which has protected the skin from wrinkling while the fetus floated in the amniotic sac.

Finally the whole birth canal from the womb to the outside (a distance of about ten centimetres) is wide enough to allow the baby to be pushed through. Before this can happen, however, the amniotic sac bursts and the liquid in it pours out (this is called **breaking the waters**). When the baby's head finally emerges, the rest of the body follows very quickly.

The baby, which is by now breathing and perhaps crying lustily, is still connected to the placenta in the womb by the umbilical cord. This is tied at two points and, quite painlessly, cut between them. A few minutes later the whole placenta separates from the womb and comes out through the vulva—this is the **after-birth**.

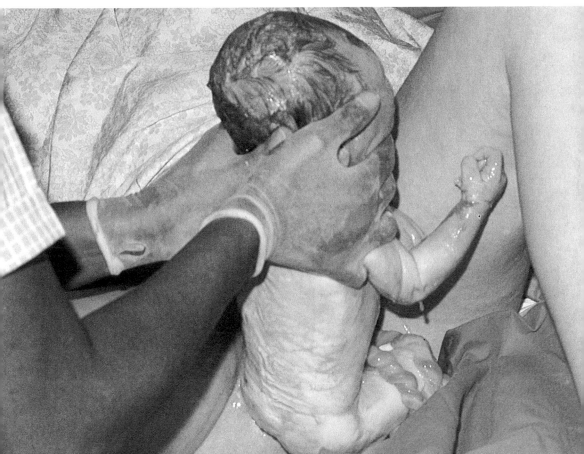

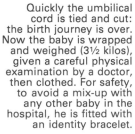
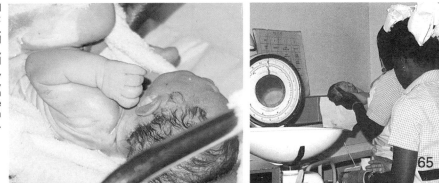

Quickly the umbilical cord is tied and cut: the birth journey is over. Now the baby is wrapped and weighed (3½ kilos), given a careful physical examination by a doctor, then clothed. For safety, to avoid a mix-up with any other baby in the hospital, he is fitted with an identity bracelet.

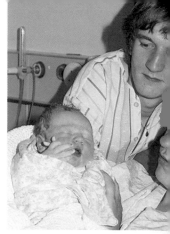

Giving birth is naturally an exhausting experience; it may also be a painful one, although anesthetics are normally used to reduce discomfort to a minimum. Most mothers find it a deeply rewarding experience, well worth all the effort and trouble of the previous nine months of pregnancy.

The mother may have her baby in a hospital or at home; she will be helped by a midwife and perhaps also by a doctor. Nowadays, the father often attends the birth, and sometimes older children.

The happy parents introduce Sarah, who is 18 months old, to her new baby brother Lee. Later the proud grandparents meet their new grandson—but by now Lee is not taking too much interest in all this activity. All he wants at the moment is a good long sleep —it's been a busy day!

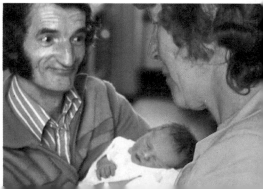

66

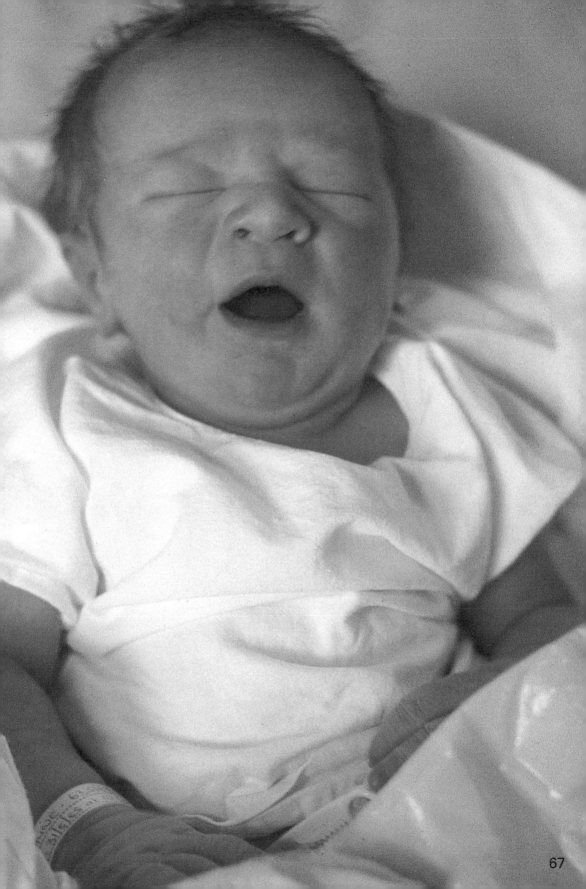

In the first months of life the baby feeds at its mother's breasts. It is completely dependent on its parents, yet holds them in its power. It already has its own personality, and its priorities are quite clear: food, comfort and security. It has a powerful voice to command the care and attention it needs: feeding every few hours, endless nappy changes, the warmth of its mother's arms. Nourished and cherished, week by week it grows bigger, stronger and better able to survive. Developing all its five senses of seeing, hearing, smelling, tasting and touching, it is exploring the exciting new world around it. It is thinking too, and developing feelings. Each day there is more to see and recognise, more to learn and remember. A lifetime of human experience—27,000 days or more—lies before it.

How the sperm cells
enter a woman's body

Sperm cells meet an ovum inside
a woman's body. They enter during
[illegible] when a man's
[illegible] woman's

[illegible]
is expelled [illegible]
the man's pen[illegible]
just below [illegible]
cells then [illegible]
ovum.

Biology lessons cover the physical facts
of growth and reproduction—essential
basic information for every young person,
but only part of the story. Now read on ....

sex

We have now looked in detail at growth (the physical changes at puberty and the way the mature sex organs work) and at reproduction (coitus and the processes of conception, pregnancy and birth).

These are the physical facts of sex: the differences between male and female (sex in its first meaning of gender) and the role each plays in reproduction (including sex in its second meaning of coitus). However— as I have already mentioned—there is a great deal more to sex than bodies, and it is now time to start looking at these other aspects of sex.

(If you are not sure of the meaning of some of the words used on this page and the next, they are explained in the glossary starting on page 74.)

- **mind, emotions and behaviour**

What are these other aspects? First, our *minds* are active: we think and talk about sex, we have ideas, we develop attitudes and we make judgments. Secondly, we have sexual *feelings* and moods: we are by turns interested, excited, confused, tempted, distressed and so on. These thoughts and feelings, which we can call the mental and emotional sides of sex, happen inside us—in our minds. They are completely private and (unless our faces give us away) invisible.

Together, however, they control our sexual *behaviour*: what we do and (equally important) what we do *not* do. Our conduct in this or that situation may be deliberate or instinctive, governed more by our thoughts or by our feelings. This is the behavioural side of sex, and it is visible: what we do and how we conduct ourselves can be seen, and judged, by everyone around us. It is the most important element in our character or personality.

As we grow up we are gradually developing attitudes and beliefs (likes and dislikes, standards of good and bad, right and wrong) about every aspect of our lives, not just about sex. However, sexual thoughts and feelings do hold a very special place in adolescence, and this is discussed under the heading New Experiences (page 81). It is also a period when we have to make a great many decisions about our sexual behaviour and relationships, and these are discussed under the headings New Responsibilities (page 91) and Life Ahead (page 104).

We have almost no control over our physical development, but we do have at least some control over our emotional, and even more over our mental, development. Learning self-control—in other words, how to control our emotions and behaviour—is a very important part of growing up.

Although we reach maturity on the sexual and physical sides without any particular effort simply by the passage of time, maturity on the emotional side does not come automatically: it has to be worked for, hard, and it can be very painful!

● different attitudes

Deeply held beliefs in politics, religion and race can lead to conflict between nations, and the feelings inspiring them may be labelled patriotism and faith or hatred and intolerance—all depending on your point of view. So it is with sex: the sexual feelings and behaviour which to some people will seem natural, normal, right and good, to others will seem unnatural, abnormal, wrong and evil.

Similarly, works of art and events which seem beautiful and inspiring to some will seem obscene and disgusting to others. For example, the two top pictures on the facing page may strike you as being interesting and funny and the next three as being beautiful—or they may all strike you as vulgar, offensive or worse.

Of course, there is universal agreement about some aspects of sex. For example, the sexual expression of love is regarded as one of the finest expressions of human feeling. On the other hand, sexual activities which take advantage of those who cannot protect themselves, which abuse a trust, or which cause harm or pain (such as **rape** and the **sexual abuse** of children) are considered wrong by everybody and are punished as crimes.

There are many areas, however, where there is substantial disagreement on sexual matters. There are arguments about what people should be allowed to see or read (arguments about **obscenity**, **pornography** and censorship, for example) or to do in public or private (such as **naturism** or nudity, or various kinds of sexual activity). There are arguments too about what kinds of relationships people should be allowed to have, and about the age at which it is sensible and safe to embark on the first physical relationship.

For some people, the only sexual activity which is morally proper is coitus within marriage, while for others any sexual activity which feels good *is* good. Other people, perhaps most, will feel that these positions are both too extreme, the one too moral and the other too immoral to be acceptable.

Even the law can be quite vague and confusing (as with the definitions of obscenity and indecency) or just inconsistent (as with the male and female ages of consent for certain sexual activities).

Sex has always been a subject of fundamental importance to human beings, and always will be. Frank representations of the sexes have been a common theme in all forms of art across the world since prehistoric times. On the facing page are a few images of sex in religion, history, art and science spanning many centuries. Reading from left to right, top to bottom:

Over 3000 years ago: these huge fertility symbols (representing the vulva and the erect penis) were sacred objects to those who carved them from rock at Land's End in Cornwall. Today there are scientific symbols for male and female: ♂ and ♀. In the East there is one ancient symbol for both, based on the egg—the Chinese interlocking yin (yolk/female) and yang (white/male): ☯

900 years ago: this is a half-metre section of the 70-metre Bayeux Tapestry depicting the story of the Norman Conquest of England in 1066. Did the needlewomen who sewed it think the cartoon at the bottom was dirty—or funny?

500 and 300 years ago: the *David*, a sculpture by Michaelangelo (in the Accademia, Florence) and the *Rokeby Venus*, a painting by Velazquez (in the National Gallery, London), are two of the greatest masterpieces in Western art: both show the nude body simply as an object of beauty.

100 years ago: at the same time as *The Kiss* by Rodin (now in the Tate Gallery, London) was being carved, the genitals of other nude statues in England were covered with stone 'fig leaves' to conform with Victorian standards of public decency. *The Kiss* was judged to be obscene by one in every 14 people polled a few years ago.

The future: this metal engraving of a naked man and woman is today several *billion* kilometres from earth! It is a part of the 'culture capsule' in Pioneer 10, launched in 1972 and now traversing our galaxy in the hope of making contact with an alien civilisation, perhaps centuries from now. What will those aliens make of their first view of human beings. . . . ?

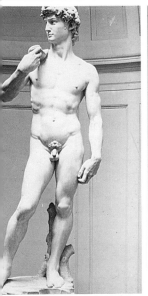

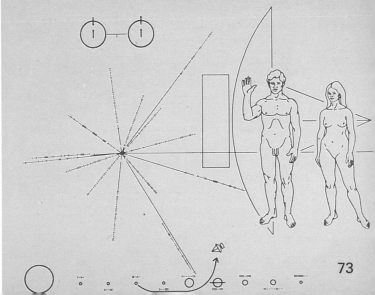

There is also much disagreement and confusion about sex education: not only in attitudes but even about the facts. There are many very unreliable sources of information (for example, playground gossip, graffiti, shoddy magazines, well-meaning but ill-informed friends). It is therefore important for you to be able to sort fact from fiction and to distinguish between good sense and nonsense.

Fortunately, there are also plenty of reliable sources. These include well-informed adults, good books (don't forget the library, and see also the foot of page 112), articles in good magazines and newspapers, educational programmes on radio and television.

● making up your mind

Wherever you encounter conflicting beliefs and points of view, in the end you will have to make up your own mind. You may find that your ideas will change as you grow older, depending on what you read, whom you talk to and what you experience yourself.

You must use your own judgment. In making up your own mind, I hope you will always try hard to sort out the facts and avoid jumping to conclusions. I hope, too, that you will always be willing to respect the beliefs and practices of other people and to recognise that, although they are different, they may well be just as sound as your own.

● the language of sex

A wide range of sexual topics appears constantly in newspapers, magazines and so on. You will often hear or read about issues under public debate and all kinds of stories about troubles which adults get themselves into. The key words in such articles are often not fully explained (or are not included) in most dictionaries. The glossary (word list) which follows therefore gives definitions not only of all the special terms which appear in this book, but also of many other terms which you may see or hear elsewhere. The full vocabulary of sex and the body includes a lot of baby-talk, euphemisms, slang, swear words and insults—but these are not included here.

You may find it useful to glance through the pages of the glossary before going on to read the rest of the book. From now on I shall be using special terms in the text without explaining them, but they are all in the glossary.

PLEASE READ THIS BEFORE USING THE GLOSSARY

1 The use of bold type in or at the end of an entry invites you to look up the term in bold, thus:

> **artificial insemination** Usually shortened to **A I**
> **change of life** Another name for **menopause**
> **fraternal twins** Explained under **twins**

direct you to **A I**, **menopause**, **twins** for the definitions. This is also the case with 'See', 'Another spelling of', etc.

2 Practically all the medical (and many general) terms used in the definitions are themselves defined in the glossary—*so do look up any term which you are not sure about.*

3 Where there are two or more terms for the same thing, the definition is given once only under the preferred term. Thus, 'genitals', 'private parts', 'reproductive organs', etc., are all shown as 'Another name for **sex organs**' and the definition is given under **sex organs**.

4 Terms which are used in the book are indicated by a page number (thus: **acne** 14) which is usually the first page on which they appear. Some very common words (like birth, sexual, etc.) have no number. The letter 'c' following the number means that the word or term appears in a caption on that page.

5 Pronunciation is indicated in sloping brackets, the stressed syllable being in bold, thus: [*ak-nee*].

6 These definitions are confined to the meanings relevant to this book; many of the words have other meanings which are not included.

7 The **index** on pages 110-111 tells you where you will find the main entries (and pictures) for each term and subject explained in the book. It also includes quite a few terms not in this glossary.

glossary

abortion, abort 24 Ending a pregnancy before the fetus is fully developed: the embryo or fetus is expelled from the womb either naturally (*spontaneous abortion* or *miscarriage*) or deliberately (*induced abortion*).

abstinence 107 Deliberately avoiding coitus or other sexual activity.

abuse, abuser 92 Misusing or mistreating; putting something to the wrong use; someone who does this. See **child abuse**, **drug abuse**, **physical abuse**, **substance abuse**.

acne *[ak-nee]* 14 Spots on face, neck and back; a skin condition common in adolescents.

activity See **sexual activity**

addiction, addict 97 Needing or relying physically or mentally on substances like alcohol, tobacco or some drugs, to the point of being uncomfortable, disturbed or desperate if deprived of them. (Also called dependency.) See also **drug addiction**.

addictive 97 Leading to **addiction**.

additives 103 Chemical substances added to foods to affect their colour or taste, or to preserve them.

adolescence 12 The process of growing up; the time of growing from child to adult; the years between the end of childhood and reaching physical maturity; includes puberty.

adolescent 12 Any young person during adolescence; also (loosely) a teenager.

adult, adulthood 10 Being physically mature, grown up; legally, 18 and over in the UK (but 17 in criminal law). See also **coming of age**.

adultery Coitus where one or both partners are married, but not to each other. (Also called extramarital sex.)

after-birth 65 The placenta when it is expelled from the womb after birth.

age of consent The lowest age at which a woman can consent, legally, to coitus; this is 16 in the UK (except N. Ireland, 17).

A I (Short for *artificial insemination*.) A medical technique for introducing semen into the vagina of a wife if the husband is fertile but impotent (*A I H, H* for husband) or, if the husband is sterile, using a donor (*AID*). Compare **I V F, surrogacy**.

AID, AIH Short for *artificial insemination by donor/husband*; explained under **A I**.

AIDS, Aids 107 (Short for *acquired immune deficiency syndrome*.) A dangerous STD which has appeared recently in Central Africa, North America and Europe. Can be transmitted by infected blood transfusions as well as sexually.

alcoholism, alcohol 97 Addiction to alcohol, a harmful drug which depresses the body's central nervous system.

allergy 103 Sensitivity of the body to certain substances being touched, swallowed or inhaled, causing unpleasant reactions such as rashes.

amniotic sac *[amny-otic]* 58c The bag made of membrane and filled with liquid in which the developing fetus floats within the womb.

amphetamines 97 A range of medical drugs often abused.

anorexia nervosa 101 (Often shortened to *anorexia*.) A disorder which sometimes occurs in adolescent girls who refuse to eat food. Without treatment they may starve.

anus *[ay-nus]* 10 The opening between the buttocks at the end of the bowel, through which feces are expelled from the body.

areola *[arry-ola]* 14 The ring of darker skin around each nipple.

artificial insemination 108 Usually shortened to **A I**.

baby See **premature baby, test-tube baby**.

balanced diet 101 Diet with the right amounts of *protein*, *fat*, *carbohydrate*, *minerals* and *vitamins*.

barbiturates 97 A range of medical drugs often abused; addictive and very dangerous.

belly 10 The part of the trunk below the navel.

bigamy, bigamist Being married to two people at once; illegal. Compare **monogamy, polygamy**.

birth Being born; delivering the fetus from the womb into the outside world. See also **after-birth, breech birth, cesarian birth, premature birth, still-birth**.

birth canal 34 The passage through which the baby leaves the womb at birth: made up of the cervix, vagina and vulva.

birth control 108 Avoiding conception by deliberately using some form of contraception. May also mean stopping a pregnancy by induced abortion. See also **family planning**.

bisexuality, bisexual *[buy-sexual]* 106 Having sexual feelings for people of both sexes. Compare **heterosexual, homosexual**.

bladder 10 The bag in which urine is stored before being expelled from the body.

body hair 14 Hair anywhere on the trunk and limbs.

bosom *[boo-zm]* 26 Another term for the **breasts**.

bowel, bowels 33c The long tube from the stomach to the anus; also called the intestine(s).

breaking the waters 65 Breaking the amniotic sac, thereby releasing the liquid in it, at the beginning of birth.

breast, breasts 14 The two external sex organs on a woman's chest which produce milk for her new-born baby.

breast-feeding 26 Feeding a baby with milk from the breasts. (Also called suckling.)

breech birth/position 62 Birth in which the baby's bottom (breech), rather than its head, faces the birth canal.

buggery 94 Another word for **sodomy**.

caesarean Another spelling of **cesarian**.

caffeine The drug in coffee and tea which is mildly stimulating. See also **drug addiction**.

calendar method Another name for the **rhythm method**.

calorie See **kilocalorie**.

cannabis 97 One of the **illegal drugs**, made from Indian hemp. (Also called marijuana.)

cap A contraceptive for women, made of thin rubber which fits over the cervix.

carbohydrate 100 The main component in foodstuffs like rice, potatoes, grains, etc., which the body turns into energy; takes various forms such as *sugar* (bad for you), *starch* (filling) and *fibre* (good for the digestion).

castration, castrate 40 Removing the testicles. (Castration is not the same as male sterilisation.) Compare **vasectomy**.

celibacy, celibate Being unmarried. (Not to be confused with chastity.)

cell, cells 15 The basic building-blocks of the body. Term also appears in egg-cell, germ-cell.

cellulose Another name for **fibre**.

cervical *[sur-vie-cl]* of the cervix.

cervix *[sur-vix]* 30 The end (or neck) of the womb which opens into the vagina.

cesarian birth *[si-zay-rian]* Birth in which the baby for some reason cannot be born through the birth canal and is therefore taken from the womb by an operation, cutting through the belly and the wall of the womb. (Also spelt caesarean.)

change of life 86 Another name for the **menopause**.

chastity, chaste 105 Not having sex before, or outside, marriage.

chauvinism, chauvinist Devotion, often extreme or unreasoning, to a cause; male sexists may be called chauvinists.

child abuse 93 Cruelty to children, whether physical or emotional; may include sexual abuse (also called child molesting).

child abuser 93 A person who abuses children, usually sexually. (Also called child molester, pedophile.)

child molesting/molester 93 Other names for **child abuse/abuser**.

chromosome *[croe-moe-soam]* 54 One of the parts of a cell which carry the genes. There are 23 pairs of chromosomes in each cell, and each chromosome contains hundreds of genes. See also **sex chromosomes**.

circumcision, circumcise *[sur-km-size]* 38 Cutting off the foreskin of the penis. A man whose foreskin is not removed is *uncircumcised*.

clitoral hood 28 The fold of the inner labia, near the top of the vulva, which protects the clitoris.

clitoris *[clit-or-iss]* 28 One of the female internal sex organs, which produces feelings of pleasure when stimulated.

cocaine 97 One of the **illegal drugs**, dangerous and addictive; made from the cocoa plant.

cohabitation Unmarried couples living together as if married.

coil A contraceptive for women (one of the I U Ds).

coitus [*co-eat-us*] 49   The act between a woman and man which is necessary for conception, in which the man puts his penis into the vagina of the woman and ejaculates. (Also called copulation, having sex, making love, sex, sexual intercourse.)

coitus interruptus   One of the 'natural' methods of contraception, in which the penis is withdrawn from the vagina before ejaculation. (Also called withdrawal.)

coming of age   Reaching legal adulthood (18 in the UK).

conceive 52   Become pregnant. See also **conception**.

conception 52   Fertilising of an ovum by a sperm; the beginning of pregnancy. The only natural method of conception is coitus, but various artificial methods are now possible in special cases: see **A I**, **I V F**. See also **fertilisation**.

condom 108   A contraceptive for men, made of very thin rubber, which fits over the erect penis; also reduces the risk of transferring STDs between partners.

congenital   From the time of birth.

contraception 108   Avoiding conception deliberately by preventing the ovum from being fertilised after coitus. There are various ways of doing this (none of them absolutely sure), including *contraceptives*, '*natural methods*' and *sterilisation*. See also **birth control**, **family planning**.

contraceptives 108   Any special devices or chemicals intended to prevent conception after coitus. They include the *cap*, *Depo Provera*, *IUDs* (the *coil* and *loop*), the *Pill* (*oral contraceptive*), *pessaries* and *spermicides*, and the *vaginal ring* and *sponge* (all for women); and the *condom* (for men).

contractions 64   Tightening of the muscles in the walls of the womb when birth is about to begin.

copulation, copulate 49   Old term for **coitus**.

cord   See **umbilical cord**.

corona [*coh-roe-nah*]   The rim round the glans of the penis.

craving 60   Feeling strong longing for something, as for special foods during pregnancy, or for drugs in drug addiction.

crotch 10   The part of the body between the legs, where the trunk forks. (Sometimes spelt crutch.)

defecation, defecate 10   Passing feces from the bowel out of the body through the anus. (Also spelt defaecate.)

dependency   Another term for **addiction**.

Depo Provera   A contraceptive for women, given by injection.

developer   See **early / late developer**.

deviation, deviant   See **sexual deviation**.

diaphragm [*dire-fram*]   One kind of contraceptive **cap**.

diet 100   Choosing particular types of food and avoiding others in order to help one's physical condition, to reduce weight or to help cure an illness. See also **balanced diet**.

discrimination, discriminate 107   Treating some people worse than others just because of their race, sex or religion. Illegal in some cases like housing, employment and education. See also **feminism**, **racism**, **sexism**.

disease   See **S T D**, **V D**.

douching [*doosh*]   Washing inside the vulva and vagina using a special syringe. Douching is not necessary and is *not* a method of contraception.

drug, drugs 97   Substances which affect the working of the body or mind in various ways. These may be good (as medicines to cure illness, reduce pain or stress, help sleep, etc.) or bad (to escape from reality, etc.). See also the following entries and **illegal drugs**.

drug abuse 97   Misusing drugs to the extent that they cause harm to the body or mind.

drug addiction / addict 97   Physical and mental **addiction** to various drugs such as *amphetamines*, *barbiturates*, *cannabis*, *cocaine*, *heroin* and *LSD*. *Alcohol* and *nicotine* are also harmful addictive drugs. (Also called drug dependency.)

drug dependency   Another term for **drug addiction**.

drugs   See **drug**.

duct   Medical term for a small tube, as in oviducts, spermatic ducts.

early developer 16   A child who starts adolescence earlier than most.

early maturer   An adolescent who reaches maturity earlier than most.

ectomorph 20   Type of physique with slender frame. Compare **endomorph**, **mesomorph**.

egg 15, **egg-cell**   Popular names for **ovum**.

ejaculation, ejaculate 16   Discharging semen from the penis at the moment of orgasm.

embryo [*em-bree-oh*] 56   The unborn baby during the first two months of growth in the womb, while it is developing from fertilised ovum to fetus.

endometrium [*endo-meet-rium*] 34   Lining of the womb on its inside surface.

endomorph 20   Type of physique with broad, muscular frame. Compare **ectomorph**, **mesomorph**.

erection 46, **erect** 26   Swelling up of the penis or clitoris until it is hard. Nipples can also become erect. See also **potency**.

erotic 46   To do with sexual love, stimulating sexual feelings.

ethnic, ethnic group 22   Belonging to a particular race or people; often used with reference to cultural activities.

eunuch [*you-nuc*] 40   A male who has been castrated.

excretion, excrete   Expelling urine or feces from the body.

exhibitionism, exhibitionist   Another term for **indecent exposure**.

external sex organs 15   The sex organs which are outside the body and therefore visible. They are, in the female, the *vulva* and *breasts*; in the male, the *penis* and *scrotum* (containing the *testicles*). (Also called genitalia, genitals, private parts, privates, pudenda.) See also **internal sex organs**.

extramarital sex   Another name for **adultery**.

facial hair 14   Hair on the face, which begins to grow at puberty.

facts of life   Popular term for the facts of sex and reproduction.

faeces   Another spelling of **feces**.

fallopian tubes 30   Another name for the **ovarian tubes**.

family planning 108   Parents deciding how many children they want in their family and also the spacing of each birth, and using contraception to make the plan happen. (Also called planned parenthood.) See also **birth control**.

fat 100   The main component (animal or vegetable) in foodstuffs like butter, cooking oils and meat fat, which the body turns into energy. Harmful if you take too much. Two main kinds: *saturated fats* (more harmful) which include animal fats and dairy products (milk, butter, cheese); and *polyunsaturated fats* (less harmful) which include fish oils and vegetable (seed and nut) oils.

feces [*fee-seez*] 10   The solid waste passed out of the body through the bowel and anus. (Also spelt faeces; the word is plural.)

female 9   Biologically, the sex which is capable of conceiving and producing babies.

female organ 28   An old name for **vagina**.

female sex organs   See **sex organs**.

feminism, feminist   Advocating the cause of equal rights for women; someone (woman or man) who does this.

fertilisation, fertilise 15   Making an ovum become able to develop into a baby by uniting a sperm with it; conceiving. See also **IVF**.

fertility, fertile 15   Being able to conceive or cause conception; fertile can also mean being able to fertilise or be fertilised. Compare **infertility**.

fetus [*fee-tuss*] 58c   The unborn baby in the womb, from the third to the ninth months of pregnancy. (Also spelt foetus.) See also **embryo**.

fibre 102   A type of carbohydrate which has no energy value but helps digestion. *High fibre* foods (fruits, vegetables, grains) are those with most fibre in them. (Also called cellulose and roughage.)

fidelity 107   Being sexually faithful; having sex with only one partner. Compare **promiscuity**.

fimbriae [*fim-bree-eye*] 30   The delicate tendrils at the end of the ovarian tubes, facing the ovaries.

flashing   Popular name for **indecent exposure**.

foetus   Another spelling of **fetus**.

foreskin 38   The loose sleeve of skin which covers the glans of the penis, and which is cut off in circumcision. (The medical name is prepuce.)

fornication, fornicate   Old term for coitus between partners who are not married.

frame 20 The shape or form of a body fixed by the skeleton. Compare **physique**.

fraternal twins 62 Explained under **twins**. (Fraternal means 'of brothers', but fraternal twins can in fact be sisters or brother and sister.)

frenulum The cord of skin holding the underside of the glans to the shaft of the penis; may be cut in circumcision.

front passage Another name for **vagina**.

gametes *[gam-eat]* 15 The special female and male sex cells which, when united, enable a new life to be created. The female gamete is the ovum, the male gametes are sperms. (Also called germ-cells.)

gay 106 Popular term for homosexual. See also **lesbian**.

gender 9 Being male or female.

gene, genes *[jean]* 54 Invisibly small structures within each cell, which contain the instructions shaping the physical and mental make-up of a human being; hundreds are carried in each chromosome. See also **heredity**.

generation 49 Various meanings: the number of years between being born and becoming a parent; all people of about the same age; parents and their children are two generations of a family.

generative organs Another name for the **sex organs**.

genetic Of the genes, to do with heredity.

genital *[jenny-tl]* 99 Relating to reproduction or the sex organs.

genital herpes *[her-peas]* 107 One of the common STDs.

genital hygiene 99 Keeping the sexual parts of the body clean and in a healthy condition.

genitalia *[jenny-tale-ya]* Another name for the **external sex organs**.

genitals 15 Another name for the **external sex organs**.

germ-cells 15 Another name for **gametes**.

gestation *[jes-]* Another name for **pregnancy**.

gland 12 Any organ which produces a special liquid (like seminal fluid), substance or hormone which the body needs. Examples: ovaries, pituitary gland, prostate gland, testicles.

glans 28, 38 The head or tip of the clitoris and of the penis.

glue sniffing 97 General name for inhaling (breathing in) the intoxicating vapours given off by the solvents in certain types of glue and many other household and industrial products; very dangerous.

gonads *[go-nads]* 48 The sex glands which produce gametes and sex hormones: the ovaries and the testicles.

gonorrhea *[gone-or-ear]* 107 One of the most common of the STDs. (Also spelt gonorrhoea.)

groin 14 Where the legs join the belly, each side of the crotch.

growing up 10 Developing from girl to woman, from boy to man; passing from childhood through puberty and adolescence to maturity (both physical and emotional).

growth spurt 12 The increase in rate of growth for a year or two which happens early in adolescence. (Also called height spurt.)

gynecology, gynecologist *[guy-ni-col-oji]* Study of the female sex organs and problems relating to them; specialist in these. (Also spelt gynaecology.)

hair See **body hair, facial hair, pubic hair**.

hallucinogens Drugs which distort the imagination, like LSD and some poisonous mushrooms; dangerous.

having sex 49 Another term for **coitus**, but is used also to mean other types of sexual activity with a partner.

height spurt 12 Another term for **growth spurt**.

heredity 54 The transmission of genes from parents to their children via the gametes. See also **inheritance**.

heritage Another name for **inheritance**.

heroin 97 One of the most dangerous and addictive of the **illegal drugs**; made from opium.

herpes See **genital herpes**.

heterosexuality, heterosexual Having sexual feelings only for people of the opposite sex. (Hetero means other.) Compare **bisexual, homosexual**.

high fibre 102 Explained under **fibre**.

homosexuality, homosexual *[hom-oh-]* 106 Having sexual feelings only for people of the same sex. (Homo means same.) Compare **bisexual, heterosexual**; see also **gay, lesbian**.

hormones 12 Special chemical substances, produced by glands, which control the development of the body and its activities. See also **sex hormones**.

hygiene *[hi-jean]* 99 Keeping healthily clean.

hymen 28 The membrane which partly covers the entrance to the vagina.

identical twins 62 Explained under **twins**.

illegal drugs 97 Drugs which must not be used or sold (unless, in some cases, prescribed by a doctor); they include *cannabis, cocaine, heroin* and *LSD*.

illegitimate Having parents who were not married to each other at the time of conception or birth; if the parents marry after the birth, their child becomes *legitimate*.

impotence, impotent Not being able to have an erection, so that a man cannot have coitus successfully; opposite of **potency**.

incest 96 Coitus between close relatives; illegal.

indecent assault 94 Inflicting sexual activity (of various kinds) on an unwilling person; illegal.

indecent exposure 94 Exposing the sex organs in public, almost always by a man to a girl or woman; illegal. (The medical term is exhibitionism; also called flashing.)

induced abortion Explained under **abortion**. (Induced means made to happen.)

infertility 108, **infertile** 40 Not being able to conceive or cause conception; opposite of fertility. (Also called sterility, sterile.)

inherit 9, **inheritance** 54 Receiving physical and mental characteristics from parents; the process of heredity. (Also called heritage.)

inner labia 28 Explained under **labia**. (The medical name is labia minora.)

insemination See **AI**.

intercourse (Short for *sexual intercourse*.) Other name for **coitus**.

internal sex organs 15 The sex organs which are inside the body. These are, in the female, the *womb, ovaries, vagina* and *clitoris*; in the male they are the *seminal vesicles* and *prostate gland*. See also **external sex organs**.

in vitro fertilisation 108 Usually shortened to **IVF**.

IUD (Short for *intra-uterine device*.) Name for any contraceptive device fitted inside the womb (such as the coil or loop).

IVF (Short for *in vitro fertilisation*.) Fertilisation of an ovum in a medical laboratory. A fertile ovum is removed from the mother, united with the father's sperm in the laboratory and then replaced for normal growth in the mother's womb. A baby conceived in this way is popularly known as a *test-tube baby*. Compare **AI, surrogacy**.

kcal Short for **kilocalorie**.

kilocalorie 100 (Usually shortened to *kcal*.) The usual measure of the energy content of foods.

kilojoule 100 (Usually shortened to *kJ*.) A measure of the energy content of food, less common than kilocalorie. There are 4.2 kilojoules to 1 kilocalorie.

kJ Short for **kilojoule**.

labia *[lay-beer]* 28 The sides of the vulva (labia is Latin for lips). The external sides are the *outer labia* and the internal ones, covering the opening of the vagina, are the *inner labia*.

labia majora / minora Medical names for *outer/inner labia*, explained under **labia**.

labour 64 The process of giving birth; delivery of a baby.

late developer 16 A child starting adolescence later than most.

late maturer An adolescent reaching maturity later than most.

legitimate Explained under **illegitimate**.

lesbian 106 A female homosexual.

life-style 106 The way of life chosen by an adult; for example marriage or cohabitation.

lips 28 Another word for **labia**.

loop A contraceptive for women (one of the IUDs).

love 72 The most powerful feelings of affection for, and devotion to, another person. In certain senses, may include sexual feelings. Impossible in a brief definition to do justice to the nature or importance of this emotion. See also **making love**.

LSD 97 (Short for *lysergide*.) One of the **illegal drugs**; an hallucinogen or psychedelic drug.

making love 49 Another name for **coitus**; but is used also to mean other types of sexual activity with a partner.

male 9 Biologically, the sex with ability to cause conception.

male member / organ Other names for **penis**.

male sex organs See **sex organs**.

malnutrition 101 Not eating enough, or not eating the right food to keep healthy. See also **nutrition**.

mammal 24 Any animal of the types which suckle their young.

marijuana 97 Another name for **cannabis**.

masturbation, masturbate 81 Causing sexual pleasure by rubbing one's sex organs.

maturity, mature 12 When the body is fully developed (physical maturity: the end of adolescence, adulthood); and— usually this is later—when the mind is fully developed (emotional maturity). See also **sexual maturity**.

meatus *[me-ay-tuss]* Opening of the urethra in the glans of the penis.

melanin 41c The brown colouring in the skin which protects it from the sun's ultra-violet rays.

membrane 28 A very thin layer of tissue such as the hymen or amniotic sac.

menarche *[men-ark-ee]* 85 The first menstruation.

menopause 86 The time in a woman's life when her periods become less regular and finally stop, usually after about 30-35 years of menstruation. (Also called the change of life.)

menses *[men-seas]* 34 The blood and tissue discharged from the vulva at menstruation.

menstrual Happening monthly; to do with menstruation.

menstrual cycle 34 The series of events which happen in the female body between the start of one menstruation and the start of the next.

menstruation, menstruate 16 Discharging blood and tissue from the endometrium through the vagina and vulva about two weeks after ovulation if the ovum is not fertilised and is therefore dead; the beginning of the menstrual cycle. (Also called having a period.)

mesomorph *[mez-oh-morf]* 20 Type of physique with broad frame. Compare **ectomorph, endomorph**.

minerals 101 Natural substances which are not animal or vegetable, some of which (like salt, iron, calcium and potassium) are necessary for good health; the very small quantities required are found in many foodstuffs.

miscarriage 24 Another name for *spontaneous abortion*, explained under **abortion**.

mixed race 22 Of parents belonging to different races.

molesting, molester See **child molesting**.

monogamy Being married to only one partner at a time. Compare **bigamy, polygamy**.

multi-cultural, multi-ethnic 22 Including several cultural or ethnic groups.

'natural' methods 108 Methods of **contraception** which do not involve any contraceptives. There are two main ones, both unreliable: *coitus interruptus* and the *rhythm method*.

naturism, naturist 72 Living without clothes as a way of life. (Used to be called nudism.)

navel 10 The small hollow above the belly on the waist line where the umbilical cord was joined to the fetus until birth. (The medical name is umbilicus.)

nicotine 98 The harmful addictive drug in tobacco.

nipple 10 The tip of a breast, at which a baby sucks milk from its mother; males also have nipples, but not for giving milk.

nocturnal emission 89 Medical term for **wet-dream**. (Nocturnal means night, and an emission is a discharge.)

nude, nudity, nudism 72 Nakedness; nudism is another word for **naturism**.

nutrition 101 The study of diet; also simply nourishment. Compare **malnutrition**.

obesity, obese 101 Very much overweight; excessively fat.

obscenity, obscene 72 Published pictures and writings are judged to be obscene if they are of such an extreme kind that they are likely to offend and disgust ordinary decent people, and may cause moral harm (in the legal phrase, 'deprave and corrupt'). Covers violence as well as sex. Compare **pornography**.

obstetrics, obstetrician Study of pregnancy and birth; specialist in these.

offence, offender See **sex offender**

oral contraceptive Another name for the **Pill**. (Oral means by mouth.)

organ 10 Any part of the body which performs one or more of the functions necessary to keep it working properly. The main organs of the head are: the brain, eyes, ears, nose, mouth, tongue. The main organs of the trunk are: the heart, lungs, stomach, kidneys, liver, bladder, intestines (bowels) and the sex organs. The largest organ of the body is the skin. (The term also appears in: female organ, male organ.) Compare **gland**.

orgasm 52 The feeling of extreme pleasure and excitement at the climax of coitus, when the muscles tense and then relax; also, for men, the moment of ejaculation.

orientation See **sexual orientation**.

orifice 28c Medical term for an opening. The external orifices of the body are the ears, nose, mouth, anus and vulva (female) or meatus in the penis (male).

outer labia 28 Explained under **labia**. (The medical name is labia majora.)

ova *[oh-vah]* 16 Plural of **ovum**.

ovarian tubes *[oh-vary-an]* 30 The two ducts (tubes) which carry ova from the ovaries to the womb; they are joined to the womb but not to the ovaries. (Also called fallopian tubes, oviducts.)

ovary, ovaries *[oh-vah-reas]* 30 The two female gonads, one on each side of the womb, which produce ova and also female sex hormones.

overweight 100 Weighing more than is healthy for one's size and age, usually because of taking too little exercise and too much food. See also **obesity**.

oviduct Another name for **ovarian tube**.

ovulation, ovulate 34 Releasing an ovum from an ovary. Usually happens about half-way through the menstrual cycle.

ovum *[oh-vum]* 15 The female gamete produced by an ovary which, if it is fertilised by a sperm, may develop into a baby. Ovum is Latin for egg, and the plural is ova. (Also called egg, egg-cell.)

pediatrics, pediatrician Study of children and their diseases; specialist in these. (Also spelt paediatrics.)

pedophilia, pedophile *[pea-doe-filly-ah; -file]* 93 Getting sexual satisfaction only by having sexual activity with a child; a pedophile is a child abuser. The great majority of pedophiles are men, and the children are more girls than boys. (Also spelt paedophilia.)

Peeping Tom 94 Popular name for a **voyeur**.

pelvis 32c The cradle of bones, at the base of the spine, forming the hips; includes the pubic bone.

penis *[pee-nis]* 10 The male sex organ which is the tube of flesh at the crotch used (when erect) in coitus, and also for urinating. The parts of the penis named in this glossary are the *corona, foreskin, frenulum, glans, meatus, root* and *shaft*.

period 34 Popular name for **menstruation**.

perversion, pervert Another word for *deviation*, explained under **sexual deviation**.

pessary A contraceptive for women in the form of a tablet containing spermicide which is placed in the vagina.

physical abuse 92 Abusing a child or adolescent physically, perhaps causing injury through violence or ill-health through neglect; may include sexual abuse.

physique *[fiz-eek]* 20 The form of the body as shaped by the flesh on the skeleton.

Pill ('the Pill') 108 The most popular type of contraceptive for women, made from hormones and taken by mouth.

pituitary gland 12 Gland, at the base of the brain, producing hormones which control growth and physical development.

placenta *[plah-centre]* 58c An organ formed during pregnancy in the lining of the womb to carry food and oxygen to the unborn baby; it is expelled from the womb after birth, when it is about one-fifth of the baby's weight. (Also called the after-birth.)

planned parenthood 108 Another name for **family planning**.

olygamy Being married to more than one person; having several wives. Compare **monogamy**, **bigamy**.

olyunsaturated fats 102 Explained under **fat**.

ornography 72 Pictures and writings intended to stimulate sexual feelings, or judged to do so. Sometimes shortened to *porn*. Compare **obscenity**.

otency, potent 40 Being able to have an erection, and therefore to have coitus; the opposite is impotence. (Also called virility.)

regnancy, pregnant 24 The time from conception to birth; a woman is pregnant when she has a baby growing in her womb. (Also called gestation.)

remarital sex Sexual activity, especially coitus, before marriage.

remature baby/birth 24 Baby weighing less than 2.5 kilos at birth, or born before the due time.

repuce *[pree-puce]* 38 Medical name for **foreskin**.

rivate parts, privates Old names for the **external sex organs**.

romiscuity, promiscuous 107 Having sex with many different partners at different times. Compare **fidelity**.

rostate gland 42 Male sex gland, situated below the bladder, producing some components of seminal fluid.

rotein *[pro-teen]* 100 The main component in foodstuffs like meat, fish and eggs, which the body turns into muscle.

rostitution, prostitute Having sex with someone for money; prostitutes may be female or male.

puberty *[pew-berty]* 14 The period when the sex organs become active; it comes early in adolescence and ends in sexual maturity.

pubic bone *[pew-bic]* 32c The front part of the pelvis immediately above the external sex organs.

pubic hair 14 The hair around the external sex organs which begins to grow during puberty.

pudenda An old name for the **external sex organs** (particularly female).

race, racial 22 Classification of people by physical differences (skin and eye colouring, type of features and hair, blood groups, etc.). See also **ethnic**, **mixed race**, **racism**.

racism, racist Belief that there are inborn physical and mental differences between races which make some superior to others; someone whose attitudes and actions are based on this mistaken belief.

rape, rapist 72 Forcing a girl or woman to have coitus against her will—a serious crime.

reproduction, reproduce 14 Producing babies, having children.

reproductive organs Another name for the **sex organs**.

rhythm method One of the 'natural' methods of contraception, based on accurate calculation of ovulation. (Also called calendar method and 'safe' period.)

root 45c The part of the penis which extends inside the body and is nearly as long as the part outside.

roughage 102 Another name for **fibre**.

'safe' period Another name for the **rhythm method**. (Period here means simply time, not menstruation.)

'safe' sex 107 Sexual activity in which the risk of transmitting an STD is reduced (but not removed) by taking sensible precautions; these include careful genital hygiene, use of a condom, and avoiding activities most likely to transfer infection.

sanitary pad 85 Pad of soft cotton-wool and tissue worn over the vulva during menstruation to absorb the menses. Compare **tampon**. (Also called sanitary towel.)

sanitary towel 85 Another name for **sanitary pad**.

saturated fats 102 Explained under **fat**.

scrotum *[scroe-tum]* 10 The bag of skin at the crotch which hangs behind and below the penis and contains the testicles.

seed 15 Popular name for **sperm**.

self-care 92 Looking after one's own health, safety and welfare.

semen *[see-men]* 16 The whitish fluid which is ejaculated when a man has an orgasm. It is composed of sperms and seminal fluid.

seminal fluid 42 The fluid produced partly by the seminal vesicles and partly by the prostate gland; when combined with sperms (which it carries and nourishes) it becomes semen.

seminal vesicles 42 Male sex glands, situated behind the bladder, which produce some components of seminal fluid and where sperms are stored after they leave the testicles.

sex 9, 49 Three main meanings: *gender*; another name for *coitus*; and the whole range of things which have to do with one's gender and *sexual activity* of all kinds. Also often used to mean *sex organs* and as a short form of *sexual*. See also 'safe' sex; extramarital sex, premarital sex; unisex.

sex abuse 93 Another name for **sexual abuse**.

sex abuser 93 Someone, usually a man, who abuses a child or adolescent sexually. See also **sexual abuse**.

sex act 49 Another name for **coitus** (in the phrase 'the sex act'), but also used to mean other types of sexual activity with a partner.

sex chromosomes 54 The pair of chromosomes in the male and female gametes which, when united at fertilisation, decide the gender of the baby.

sex crimes Any sexual activity which is (or, depending on circumstances, may be) against the law. Examples: *child abuse*, *incest*, *indecent assault*, *indecent exposure*, *rape*, *sodomy*. See also **sex offender**.

sex disease Another name for any kind of **S T D**.

sex drive 81 The powerful sexual instinct or urge which from time to time becomes a need for stimulation and satisfaction in some sexual activity. See also **sexuality**.

sex hormones 30 Hormones produced by the gonads and some other glands which control activity of the sexual system and sexual functions of the body.

sexism, sexist Discrimination against the opposite sex on the grounds that yours is superior—usually men against women. Compare **chauvinism**, **feminism**.

sex offender Someone (usually but not always male) who commits a sex offence or crime. See also **sex crimes**.

sex organs 15 All the organs and glands which are designed for reproduction. The female sex organs are the *vulva*, *clitoris*, *vagina*, *womb*, *ovaries* and *breasts*; the male sex organs are the *penis*, *testicles*, *seminal vesicles* and *prostate gland*. (Also called generative organs, genitalia, genitals, private parts, privates, reproductive organs, sexual organs.) Term also appears in: external sex organs, internal sex organs.

sexual Of or to do with sex in all its meanings. The word may be used in particular phrases like those below (and those above where *sexual* may be substituted for *sex*); or it may be used (as it often is in this book) in front of general words like ability, emotions, feelings, partner, power, thoughts, etc.

sexual abuse 72 Abuse of a child or adolescent involving some sexual activity; the person doing this is called a sex abuser.

sexual activity 72 General term for all types of physical activity of a sexual kind, including not only coitus and masturbation but also petting, necking and other activities which fall short of coitus or orgasm.

sexual deviation/deviant 106 Sexual activity considered to be unnatural in a particular society at a particular time—although what is considered unnatural in one place or time may be accepted as natural in another: customs vary and ideas change. However, some practices like child abuse and getting sexual pleasure from inflicting pain or humiliation are considered to be deviations almost everywhere. (Also called sexual perversion.) See also **sexual orientation**.

sexual intercourse 49 (Sometimes shortened to *intercourse*.) Another name for **coitus**, but is used also to mean any sex act in which a man's penis enters his partner, with or without orgasm. (Also called sexual relations.)

sexuality 81 The part of one's personality which has to do with sex, and one's sexual interests and behaviour. See also **sexual orientation**.

sexually transmitted disease 107 Usually shortened to **S T D**.

sexual maturity 14 Having the ability to reproduce, achieved by the end of puberty. See also **maturity**.

sexual orientation 106 The direction taken by one's sexuality, particularly in relation to sexual preferences in such things as the gender and number of partners, their age, their physical characterstics and features, and so on. The orientation may also be deviant. See also **sexual deviation**.

sexual perversion Another term for **sexual deviation**.

sexual relations   Another term for **sexual intercourse**.

sexual system 33c   The physical arrangement of sex organs in the body which enables them to do their job. (The female and male sexual systems are shown together on page 48.)

shaft 38c   The part of the penis between the glans and crotch.

skeleton 12   The complete assembly of bones in the body (350 at birth, 206 when physically mature) making the frame on and within which fit the flesh, muscles, organs, etc.

smegma 99   Soapy white substance produced around the corona of the penis, under the foreskin.

sodomy 94   Penetration of the anus by the erect penis. (Also called buggery.)

solvents 97   Types of chemical used in many glues and sprays whose vapour is intoxicating, with physical and mental effects rather like those of alcohol. See also **glue sniffing**.

sperm, sperms 15   The male gamete produced by the testicles, necessary to fertilise an ovum. (The word sperm is sometimes used to mean sperms in the plural. Also called seed. The medical name is spermatozoon, plural spermatozoa.)

spermatic ducts   Another name for **sperm tubes**.

spermatozoon, spermatozoa 38   The medical names for **sperm, sperms**.

spermicide   Any substance (cream, foam, jelly or pessary) which kills sperms; used together with a condom or cap (or in a vaginal sponge) as a contraceptive.

sperm tubes 42   The two ducts (tubes) which carry sperms from the testicles to the seminal vesicles. (Also called spermatic ducts. The medical name is vasa deferens.)

spontaneous abortion   Miscarriage, explained under **abortion**.

spurt   See **growth spurt**.

starch 100   A type of carbohydrate, found in many foodstuffs but particularly in grains, rice, potatoes, etc.

stature 18   Natural height.

S T D 107   (Short for *sexually transmitted disease*.) Any kind of infection or disease which can be passed from an infected person to a partner during coitus or many other types of sexual activity. They include *Aids*, *genital herpes*, *gonorrhea*, *syphilis*. Several STDs can do serious and permanent harm if they are not properly treated and cured; some can also be passed to unborn babies. (The old name was VD.)

sterilisation, sterilise 108   Making infertile (sterile); the only permanent method of **contraception**; an operation to make a fertile man or woman infertile. See also **vasectomy**.

sterility 107, **sterile** 40   Other words for **infertility, infertile**.

still-birth, still-born 24   Baby dead at birth.

stimulation, stimulate 26   Making active, exciting, arousing.

substance abuse 92   Misusing substances like alcohol, tobacco and some kinds of drugs and solvents. See also **abuse, addiction, drug abuse**.

suckle   Another term for **breast-feed**.

surrogacy, surrogate   If a woman has something wrong with her womb so that an ovum cannot develop normally in it, it is possible for a fertilised ovum to be removed from her and placed in the womb of another woman, called the surrogate mother. (Surrogate means substitute.) The fetus develops in the surrogate womb and is born in the normal way, and the baby is then taken over by the real mother. This is a new medical technique which raises serious legal and ethical problems. So far it is very rare. Compare **A I**, **I V F**.

sweat 14   Salty moisture produced by the skin; increased by hard work, heat, fever, emotion, etc.

syphilis *[sif-ill-iss]* 107   One of the most dangerous STDs.

tampon 85   Small cylindrical pad of cotton-wool and tissue worn inside the vagina during menstruation to absorb the menses. Compare **sanitary pad**.

tar 98   The substance in tobacco which, when smoked, harms the lungs and, when chewed and swallowed, harms other parts of the body.

teenager 12   A young person in the 'teen years, between the ages of 12 and 19. See also **adolescent**.

testes *[tess-teas]* 38   Medical name for **testicles** (singular testis).

testicles 10   The two male gonads, in the scrotum, which produce sperms and also male sex hormones. (The medical name is testes.) See also **undescended testicle**.

testis   Singular of **testes**.

test-tube baby   Explained under **I V F**.

tissue 28   Similar cells joined together to make up one of the substances of which the body is composed, such as muscle, fat, skin, bone.

tobacco 97   The plant used in cigarettes, etc., containing nicotine, which is poisonous and addictive, and tar, which causes cancer and other dangerous diseases. Inhaling its smoke (directly or from other people smoking) or chewing it are both harmful.

tranquillisers 97   A range of medical drugs often abused.

trunk 14   Main part of the body, minus the head and limbs.

tubes   See **ovarian tubes, sperm tubes**. (The medical term is ducts.)

twins 62   Two babies which grow in the womb together and are born one after the other. They may be *identical twins* (from the same fertilised ovum which splits) or *fraternal twins* (from two different ova fertilised at the same time).

umbilical cord *[um-bill-ical]* 58c   The tube which joins the placenta to the fetus, through which the mother supplies it with the food and oxygen it needs to develop.

umbilicus   Medical name for **navel**.

uncircumcised 38   Explained under **circumcision**.

undescended testicle 40   Testicle remaining inside the groin at birth, rather than having already descended into the scrotum.

unisex   Popular term describing goods and services suitable for either sex (for example, certain types of clothing, hairdressers).

urethra *[you-reeth-rah]* 10   The tube from the bladder along which urine passes out of the body, through the vulva or penis.

urine, urinate 10   The yellowish liquid waste stored in the bladder; expelling it from the body through the urethra.

uterus 30   Medical name for the **womb**.

vagina *[vaj-eye-nah]* 28   The female sex organ which is the expandable passage leading from the cervix to the vulva; used in menstruation, in birth and in coitus. (Also called the female organ, front passage.)

vaginal sponge   A contraceptive for women; the sponge, filled with spermicide, is fitted in the vagina.

vasa deferens   Medical name for the **sperm tubes** (the singular is *vas* deferens).

vasectomy   The operation for sterilisation of a man; it involves cutting and blocking the two sperm tubes in the scrotum.

V D (Short for *venereal disease*.) 107   Old name for any **S T D**.

venereal diseases *[ven-ear-ial]* 107   Usually shortened to **V D**.

vernix 64c   The protective wax which is thinly coated over the skin of the fetus until birth.

vesicles   See **seminal vesicles**.

vestibule   The internal part of the vulva; entrance to the vagina.

virgin, virginity *[ver-jin]*   Someone who has not yet had coitus. When people do so for the first time they are said to lose their virginity.

virility, virile 40   Other names for **potency, potent**; also, more generally, male sexual power.

vitamins 101   Special substances in many foodstuffs, which are necessary to good health; known by letters (A, B, C, D, E, K).

voyeurism, voyeur   Spying on others for sexual excitement. (Also called Peeping Tom.)

vulva *[vull-vah]* 10   The female sex organ which is the narrow opening in the crotch used (like the vagina) in menstruation, in coitus and in birth; also used in urinating; the entrance to the vagina. The parts of the vulva named in this glossary are: the *outer labia*, *inner labia*, *vestibule*, *clitoris*, *clitoral hood*, and the openings of the *urethra* and *vagina*.

waters   See **breaking the waters**.

wet dream 89   An ejaculation during sleep, common during puberty and adolescence. (Also called nocturnal emission.)

withdrawal   Two meanings. Referring to drug abuse, means giving up drugs after becoming an addict. In contraception, another term for **coitus interruptus**.

womb *[woom]* 28   The female sex organ in which a baby grows for nine months through all the stages from fertilised ovum to embryo to fetus to birth. (The medical name is uterus.)

new experiences

There are two special new developments at puberty which I have already explained: menstruation and ejaculation. There is one other physical experience which I have not yet explained: this is masturbation (see page 88), which many children discover at puberty, although many have already discovered it during childhood.

Girls and boys have a lot of questions about all these, and so in this section I shall answer the most frequent of their questions. (Because these matters are very personal and private, this section is not illustrated as the previous ones on growth and reproduction were.) These, however, are not the only new experiences of adolescence. We grow up in our minds just as we do in our bodies, and the changes taking place there can be a good deal more mysterious, confusing and even shattering than the physical ones.

The transition from childhood to sexual maturity takes perhaps three or four years, and from there to full physical maturity takes as long again. Full emotional maturity, however, takes even longer to achieve; in other words, most people do not reach emotional adulthood until a few years after they are physically adult.

• the opposite sex

Before puberty, most girls and boys are not particularly interested in the opposite sex: girls usually make friends with girls and boys with boys, and it is quite common for children to take part in sexual play with friends of the same sex. About the time of puberty, however, girls and boys gradually find themselves becoming more interested in the subject of sex.

Both begin to think more about their appearance, to wonder if others find them attractive, and to find others attractive in a physical way. They are becoming aware of their **sexuality**, of the fact that they have a **sex drive** and that sex is a fundamental part of their lives.

• sexuality

Sexuality is the combination of our gender and our sexual interests and behaviour. It makes up the part of our personality which has to do with sex, and is expressed in our relationship with others.

We do not choose our sexuality: partly it is fixed in our bodies from birth, partly it is formed in our early years while we are still unaware of it, and we discover it as we grow up. We may discover that sex has the same sort of importance for us as it has for most other people—or perhaps it has a greater or lesser interest for us than for others. We may find that we are more active sexually, or less, than others.

We will certainly find out how and where our sexual interests focus, and these can be very different for different people. For example, some will find that their interest focuses early and clearly on a single partner so that eventually (if the feelings are mutual) this may turn out to be a life-long partnership. Others will find that they fall in and out of love often and rapidly. Others will not discover love for years, or perhaps ever.

We express our sexuality in many very different feelings and attitudes. These range, for example, from love, passion and infatuation to lust, jealousy and obsession; from pleasure, satisfaction and joy to modesty, embarrassment and shame.

We have to come to terms with our own sexuality: we cannot achieve maturity until we learn to accept ourselves as we are. Of course, as I have said, we can control our feelings and emotions to some extent, but there are many aspects of our personality that are more or less fixed by the time we become aware of them.

We may, and should, try to improve what we do not like in ourselves, but we have to be realistic about our limitations and potential. In the same way, we can make efforts to improve our appearance (by taking care with cosmetics, hair and clothes, and by keeping in good shape, for example) but only within limits. It is foolish to try to cheat ourselves about what these limits really are.

Our happiness in adult life depends to a very large extent on our ability to come to terms with the reality of the way we are—physically, mentally and emotionally. The extent to which we accept and then make the best of what we are is a good measure of our emotional maturity.

- **the sex drive**

  We all have some powerful physical and emotional urges and instincts inside us which need to be satisfied and which, to that extent, influence our behaviour. Some of these are irresistible, like hunger and thirst and sleep; others, like sex, can be resisted, although perhaps not easily.

  The sex drive is the uninvited urge which from time to time becomes a need for some sexual stimulation and satisfaction—sexual, because the feelings aroused and satisfied are centred largely in the sex organs. The sex drive becomes important from puberty on. It is at its strongest for most men in early adulthood, and for most women a few years later. We do not know for sure the reason for this difference.

- **confusion of feelings**

  It is natural to be sensitive about these new feelings and emotions, and to feel both proud and shy at the same time—proud of the evidence of growing up (the first bra or the first shave, for example), shy about other people noticing and perhaps teasing. This sort of confusion of feelings is quite typical of the uncertainties of adolescence. It is a time when nothing is sure, nothing stands still and (or so it may sometimes seem) nothing can be relied on.

The stability, comfort and security of childhood have gone and can never be brought back. For many young people this is very hard to accept: childhood is deeply missed, leaving behind a strong sense of loss and the unfairness of life. At the same time, acceptance into the adult world is still a long way off. Your body tells you that you are no longer a child, but you are still being treated as one.

The emotional upheavals of these years can be tough. Feelings are more intense than ever before and they can change without warning or obvious cause. Confidence and doubt, enthusiasm and boredom, sociability and loneliness, all will grip you in turn. Happily, the good times outweigh the bad, and the best are lived with an intensity of enjoyment and discovery which you will perhaps never match again in later life.

- **the struggle for independence**

Children are completely dependent on their parents (or guardians) for just about everything, while adults have to be able to look after themselves: they have become independent. One aspect of growing up from child to adult, and an extremely important one, is therefore the achievement of independence; in particular, independence from parents.

There are confusions and conflicts of feelings here too. Adolescents may find themselves torn between their growing need for independence and the desire to hang on to the comfort and security which they have enjoyed as children. Parents who during childhood were providers and protectors now in adolescence seem to become opponents and oppressors. In fact the parents have changed little (although they *are* behaving differently), while the growing adolescent is changing a great deal.

Adolescents—naturally—want freedom to run their own lives, do what they want to and see whom they want to when they want to. Parents— just as naturally—want to protect them from the very real dangers which they may encounter as they spread their wings more.

Manners and habits, tidiness, staying out late, clothes and hair-styles, make-up and ear-rings, smoking and drinking and swearing, schoolwork and household chores, the choice of friends—these and many more major and minor matters may be causes of conflict.

It is not easy for one generation to understand the attitudes and behaviour of another: goodwill is essential, even if it may be in short supply at times.

- **new needs**

So you can see that adolescents develop needs which they did not have as children: the need for knowledge, the need for extra understanding and goodwill from parents and others, the need for independence, the need for new and close relationships outside the family, the need for sexual expression. There are other new needs as well, just as important.

Puberty often brings new feelings of modesty and a need for privacy. As a child, for example, you probably thought nothing of running around naked. Now you want to be able to lock the bathroom door, to have other members of the family knock before entering your bedroom, to have your own private—absolutely private—space in the home, to be able to be completely alone when you want to.

There is a continuing need to be able to make mistakes without the world coming to an end. You need to be able to decide things for yourself, even if this sometimes means ignoring the best of advice and making an obvious blunder: often there is no better way to learn a useful lesson.

● **developing your personality**

All the experiences of adolescence—the bad ones as well as the good— are valuable in building your new, adult personality. You are learning to exercise judgment: thinking things through, working out consequences, weighing up choices and priorities. You are learning to explain yourself to others as well as to yourself: what you think, how you feel, why you want to do this or that. You are learning how to see things from other people's points of view, and how to compromise.

These are only examples of the skills which you are developing without realising it. They are all helping you to learn to control your feelings— the self-control which I have already talked about.

Remember that most people value the personality of their friends much more than their looks: such positive qualities as kindness, sincerity, good humour and thoughtfulness count for a lot more than shape or colour, curves or muscles!

● **first love**

Finally, a word about the first experience of love—or of what may seem to be love. This is likely to happen without warning (just like the first menstruation or ejaculation) in the early years of adolescence. Suddenly you find yourself experiencing a great upsurge of very intense feeling, probably for someone older and of either sex—maybe someone in a higher form or a teacher or a pop star. These feelings take total control of you and, while they last, nothing else in the world seems to matter.

It is impossible to describe the feeling—but I can assure you that when it happens you will recognise it. This is an infatuation, a crush (sometimes called puppy love), and it will pass.

We do not know what triggers the emotion of love; all we really know is that it happens in the mind and is completely unpredictable. It may have something to do with sexual fantasies (day dreams) which everyone has and in which images of an 'ideal' lover may develop. It is romantic to imagine that there is only one true love for you in the whole world, but it is not very realistic: we do, after all, only meet a very few of the hundreds of millions of possible partners before falling in love with one!

menstruation

The first menstruation is the first real sign of womanhood, a cause for pride and an important event in a girl's life. Menstruation (which I described on page 34) is a natural process, not an illness, and it is certainly not something to be frightened or ashamed or embarrassed about. It is not something that a woman has any choice about, and it is not pleasurable, so it is not like ejaculation for men.

Women today take a positive attitude to menstruation, not treating it as a 'curse' any more but accepting it simply as an essential part of being a woman.

It is still believed in some societies and religions, however, that menstrual blood is 'dirty' because it is cleaning out the body, and that women are 'unclean' when they are menstruating. (It was surely men and not women who established these beliefs!) Medically, of course, this is all completely untrue. Menstrual blood is simply blood (the amount of tissue in it from the lining of the womb is very small, and the ovum itself is no bigger than a pinhead) and it is no more 'unclean' than sweat.

Because menstruation is such an important subject, and because there is so much nonsense talked, all girls (and boys) need to be well-informed about it. Here are the answers to the questions which I am asked most often.

- *When should a girl begin menstruation?* There is no 'right' age. Most girls begin menstruating when they are about 13 years old, but it is quite normal to begin as early as 9 or as late as 17. The first menstruation has a special name: the **menarche**.

- *How much blood is lost during a period?* The amount of blood lost at each period is much less than most people think. Usually it is only about half a small cupful: this is only a tiny part of the five or six litres in the average adult body, and is replaced very quickly.

Because the blood lost during menstruation comes out of the vulva only a little at a time during several days, it is necessary to wear some type of **sanitary pad** (or **sanitary towel**) during the whole period. The simplest type is a pad of cotton wool or tissue worn over the vulva. When it has absorbed as much blood as it can, it is thrown away and a new one put on.

Many women prefer a much smaller type called a **tampon**, which is worn inside the vagina. Tampons can sometimes cause irritation or infection, so it is important to use them with great care.

- *How long should periods last?* The length of periods (that is, the number of days of bleeding) varies a lot from woman to woman, and each woman's own periods may vary from one to the next. The bleeding may go on for as little as three days or as much as eight days: about five days is common.

If there is more blood than usual, we say that the period is 'heavy', and if there is less than usual it is 'light'. The first few periods are often either very light or very heavy. You may menstruate for some time before you find how much bleeding is normal for you, and you will find that a period may be light or heavy at any time.

- *Does bleeding just start without warning?* Sometimes. The menstrual cycle is controlled by sex hormones produced by the ovaries, and these hormones make a number of different things happen in the body at different times in the cycle. These vary from one woman to another: some may notice a tenderness in the breasts or some discomfort in the lower belly, others a small increase in weight (the body retains more water than normal) or the appearance of a few pimples or spots.

- *How often should periods come?* The word menstruation comes from an old word meaning month, but menstruation is not really monthly in the sense of calendar months, which vary between 28 and 31 days. No woman has her periods on exactly the same date each month. The menstrual cycle— counted from the first day of one period to the first day of the next—varies a lot: perhaps from 21 days for some women to 36 days for others. For most women it is about 27 to 29 days.

During the first few months of menstruation, periods do not always come regularly. A girl may have one or two periods and then none for several weeks or even months. Usually her periods are coming fairly regularly after a year or so, but even then the next period may come early or late, perhaps by a day or two, or perhaps by several days. This may be because of some slight illness, or even simply some worry or excitement. There may also occasionally be a little bleeding between periods.

Once a woman has begun to have periods fairly regularly, she will usually go on like this for perhaps 30 to 35 years. Then the periods become less regular and finally they stop altogether. This time of her life is called the **change of life**, or **menopause**.

The same days of menstrual bleeding which are marked on the calendar on page 87 are shown by the pink bars on the chart below. The days of each menstrual cycle are counted on the orange strip underneath the days of each month. As you can see, in this example the cycles started on 21 January, 19 February and 20 March (*not* the same day each month). Each of the two complete cycles lasted 29 days; there were four days of bleeding in the first and five days in the second. This chart also shows the likely time of ovulation in each cycle—about 14 days before the start of the next cycle (see the top two paragraphs on page 87).

	JANUARY															FEBRUARY											
days of month	10	11	12	13	14	15	16	17	18	19	20	21	22	23	24	25	26	27	28	29	30	31	1	2	3	4	5	6	7	8	9	10	11
MENSTRUAL CYCLE												1	2	3	4	5	6	7	8	9	10	11	12	13	14	15	16	17	18	19	20	21	22
												PERIOD						OVULATION																

- *What is the difference between menstruation and ovulation?* Ovulation (as I explained on page 34) is the release of a fertile ovum from one of the ovaries every four weeks or so, and menstruation is the discharge of the dead ovum about two weeks later. As the menstrual cycle is measured from the beginning of bleeding in one period to the beginning of bleeding in the next, ovulation—the release of the *next* ovum—usually comes about half way through the cycle (as you can see on the chart below).

  The ovum is usually fertile (able to be fertilised by a sperm) only for a day or two after leaving the ovary: in other words, about half way between one period and the next. It is very difficult to know *exactly* when it is fertile, however, because everything is happening out of sight and the timing of each cycle may be a bit different from the one before.

- *Is there anything I should avoid doing during a period?* People may tell you that you must not have a bath or wash your hair during a period; or that you must avoid energetic exercise like playing games or swimming. None of this is right: there is no medical reason for you to stop any of your usual activities just because you have a period. Nor is there any need to use any special soaps or sprays.

- *Is menstruation painful?* Many women feel some discomfort during a period and a few will be unlucky enough to feel some faintness, sickness or cramps for a time. Worrying about pain can, of course, make it worse! However, most women treat periods as the natural and normal events they are, and simply get on with their daily lives.

Here a woman is marking her calendar with a circle for every day on which she has any menstrual bleeding. As you can see, all through the year she has had four or five days of bleeding at each period, and the cycles have been 28 or 29 days. This is only an example, of course, and many women do not have such regular menstrual cycles. It is easy to keep a record like this, and you will find it helpful to learn the pattern of your own cycles. You can devise your own system to indicate days of heavy and light bleeding, and so on.

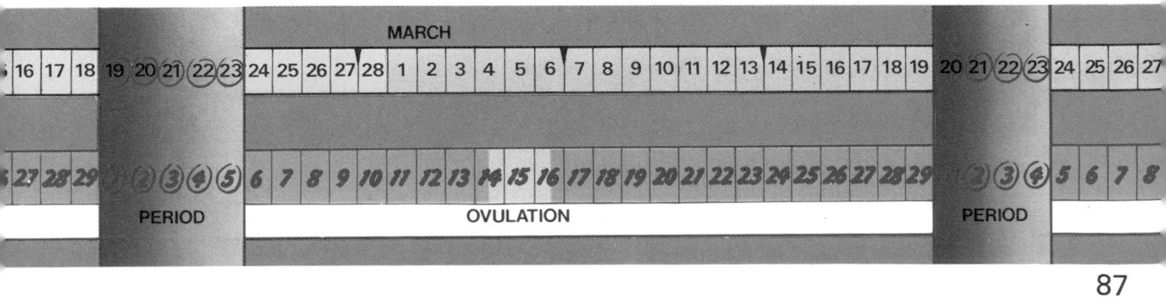

masturbation

We have seen that when a man and woman have sex, the sex organs become very sensitive, giving a feeling of great pleasure. It is possible to produce some of this feeling in other ways than by having sex with a partner. Each of us can give ourselves pleasure by rubbing or stroking our own sex organs: this is called **masturbation**.

Most children play with their sex organs when they begin to explore their body at an early age: they find that this feels good and so discover masturbation for themselves.

A girl masturbates by rubbing her vulva and clitoris, or by putting fingers inside the vagina, sometimes until a climax is reached. A boy usually masturbates by rubbing his penis with his hand; this becomes erect and (after reaching puberty) he will usually then have an orgasm and ejaculate. Sometimes children playing together masturbate each other.

- *Is masturbation natural?* Yes. It is completely natural and normal for children and young people to masturbate. It seems to be one of nature's ways of preparing the developing body for adulthood. Particularly during adolescence, when the sex drive is very strong, masturbation is a natural way to relax and get rid of sexual tension (that is, feelings of stimulation and pressure like the feelings you get before an orgasm). It is also a normal part of sex for adults as well as young people.

- *Is masturbation harmful?* No. In the past, many people had very strange ideas about masturbation. Young people were warned by their elders—most of whom themselves must have masturbated at some time—that it could cause all sorts of problems, ranging from bad breath, bedwetting and acne to infertility, baldness and even blindness. However, we know now that all these stories are just nonsense: masturbation does no harm at all.

  There is, however, one harmful effect which can arise. Some children are scolded or even punished for masturbating and are thereby made to feel ashamed and guilty. This is doubly sad and unfair. There is no cause to feel guilty about masturbating; but worse, for some people the feeling of guilt may go deep and have a lasting harmful effect on their future sex life.

- *Is masturbation necessary?* Not at all: many girls and boys never feel any desire to masturbate, and this too is perfectly normal. There are no rules or medical reasons to say you *must* masturbate, any more than there are any to stop you doing so if you wish to. It is a choice and decision which you are completely free to make for yourself.

- *Does masturbation leave any visible signs?* No. It may stretch the hymen, but so can vigorous exercise, and so a stretched hymen is no proof of masturbating; nor are large inner labia. Masturbation is a private activity, so no-one can know about it if you do not want them to.

ejaculation

The first ejaculation is the first real evidence of manhood. Orgasm is the most exciting physical feeling that most men ever experience, and a man will have many thousands of ejaculations in his lifetime. That is the way nature has made us. It is not surprising, therefore, that ejaculation (which I described on page 46) and the things that go with it— semen, orgasm, erection—are very important subjects for every man and boy.

- *What happens at ejaculation?* At ejaculation the semen is usually discharged in a few spurts at intervals of a second or
so, perhaps with a lot of force, perhaps with very little. The amount of semen produced at ejaculation is quite small: usually it is only about a small teaspoonful, but it may be less or a lot more. The semen itself is usually thickish, but it may be very thick or quite thin. In any case, each ejaculation will contain many many millions of sperms.

- *How often is it safe to ejaculate?* As often as you want to. There is no danger, and there are no rules which have to be obeyed, so it is a matter for each individual to decide for himself. Some men are a lot more active than others: for some it is normal to have an orgasm once a week, while for others once or twice a day, or even several times a day, is normal.

You may hear people say that you will 'use up' all your semen and become sterile if you ejaculate too often. This is complete nonsense because once you begin to produce semen during puberty you will continue to do so for the rest of your life—although the amount will reduce as you get older.

Ejaculation takes a lot of effort, and a man usually feels tired or exhausted immediately afterwards. It takes time to recover from an orgasm, and many men cannot have another for several hours. Some can ejaculate again after only a few minutes, but the amount of semen (and, of course, sperms) in the second orgasm will be less.

- *Is it harmful not to ejaculate?* No. You cannot catch any disease or become ill even if you do not ejaculate for a long time.

You cannot stop your testicles from producing semen, however, and so even if you are not masturbating the semen will be discharged by itself from time to time. This is called a **wet dream** (or **nocturnal emission**): that is, you ejaculate while you are asleep. It may happen while you are having a sexual dream, and you may wake up just as you ejaculate, or just after.

Having a wet dream may cause some embarrassment if sheets or clothing are marked with semen (stains wash off easily), but it is completely natural and does no harm at all. Almost every boy has wet dreams at one time or another, and none has ever been harmed by it. Like masturbation, this is a natural process and there is no need to feel guilty or worry about it.

With acknowledgments to the
Health Education Council, who
used this idea in a 1970 poster
with the message: 'Would you
be more careful if it was
you that got pregnant?'

new responsibilities

Adolescence is a period of increasing responsibilities, to others as well as to ourselves. The responsibilities to ourselves include keeping healthy and protecting ourselves from abuse of all kinds; these subjects are dealt with in this section in the chapters on self-care, hygiene and diet (pages 92-103).

We have responsibilities to others in all aspects of our lives, of course, but here we shall be considering only those which are going to be involved in our future physical and sexual relationships.

The most important fact that all young people must understand fully is this: from the moment a girl begins menstruating she is producing ova which can be fertilised; in the same way, from the moment a boy begins ejaculating he is producing sperms which can fertilise an ovum. (The very first ova and sperms may not in fact be fertile, but they *may* be: there is no way that you can tell, and you cannot afford to take any chances at all.)

So if any girl who has reached the age of menstruating has sex with any boy who has reached the age of ejaculating, *that sex act may lead to pregnancy.*

Being *able* to become a mother or father just because the sex organs have begun to work does not mean being *ready* to become a parent. Very few young people are emotionally or practically ready to take on the serious responsibilities of being a parent while they are still growing up.

Any relationship which may develop into a sexual one is therefore to be taken very seriously indeed, and it is particularly important for you to be clear about the rights and responsibilities which you both have.

You have rights yourself—to your privacy and independence, for example, your dignity and free will. However powerful the feelings, however close a relationship you have, *no partner has the right to pressure or force you to do anything which you do not want to — and you have no rights over others.* You do have a responsibility to respect the rights of others in just the same way that you expect them to respect yours.

Relationships in which one of the partners is trying to change the other, for whatever reason, or in which one partner feels imposed on or manipulated, are likely to breed insecurity, distress or anxiety. You must never assume that your partner's feelings and needs are the same as yours.

Relationships which have any chance of flourishing and lasting involve giving as well as taking, but on a shared basis of equality: there must be mutual caring, compromise, sympathy and commitment.

The day will come when you will want to embark on a sexual relationship. *You have an absolute responsibility to your future partner and to yourself not to attempt to start a physical relationship until you are quite sure that both of you understand exactly what you are getting into.*

is could really happen, what do you think he would be feeling?
should not be in too much of a hurry to make assumptions about
opposite sex and the responsibilities of entering a sexual relationship.

self-care

As you grow up, you have to take more and more responsibility for looking after yourself, although of course adults are still around to help. You have already learnt to deal with various hazards of life such as danger on the roads or in the water, or treating fire, gas and electricity with respect. There are other hazards which are equally harmful but may be much less obvious. Indeed, there are some experiences which are actually enjoyable at the time but nevertheless pose a real threat to your safety, health and peace of mind.

It is very important to be alert to these in order to avoid them: you need to be able to recognise the danger signals, to understand the risks and to know how to avoid them.

We are going to look at three main types of hazard: **physical abuse, sexual abuse** and **substance abuse**.

Substance abuse is the overall term for misusing substances like alcohol, tobacco, solvents and illegal drugs. The responsibility for the misuse is entirely your own, and you can therefore avoid it in the first place. Physical and sexual abuse are different because they are things which are done to you—but you can nevertheless take steps to avoid them.

- **your rights**

  Even as a child and teenager you have important rights. For example, your body belongs to you and you have the right to decide what to do with it. Adult society has the duty to look after your health and welfare—and therefore to protect you from avoidable dangers—but in real life these rights are not always assured.

  Most adults have the welfare of young people at heart, but some do not: for many reasons some people are ready to deceive, exploit and even harm you—if you let them. You therefore have to take sensible precautions to protect yourself.

  There is no magic way to tell you whom you can trust. Kind faces, good clothes, official jobs and so on are not always a reliable guide. Even people you admire may try to tempt or force you to do things which will harm you.

- **physical abuse**

  Some adults who have serious problems themselves are violent to children, and some of them are fathers or mothers. Physical abuse is *violence*: it is quite different from reasonable punishment (although you may find it hard to see the difference if you do not think you have done wrong).

  If you really believe that you are the victim of violence, there is something practical that you can and should do about it. No matter who the attacker is—bully, relative, parent, whoever—you must seek help from a trusted adult as soon as you safely can. (See the bottom panel on page 95.)

- **sexual abuse**

  Sexual abuse (also called **sex abuse** or **child abuse** or **child molesting**) is not usually violent: it is much more likely to be gentle and apparently harmless. People who abuse children or adolescents in this way are called **sex abusers** or **child abusers** or **child molesters** (or sometimes **pedophiles**).

  Here are some basic facts which you should know about sex abuse:
  - *you* are at risk—girl or boy, child or teenager, at any age
  - most sex abusers are men—but some are teenagers and some are women
  - victims are just as likely to be abused by people *they already know*—abusers may be anyone around, relatives or even members of the family
  - many sex abusers victimise not just one but *many* young people
  - any person who abuses children or adolescents is committing a crime.

  The danger of being sexually abused is real and widespread enough for *all* young people to be very careful. People who think 'it can't happen to me' should understand that it can happen to anyone.

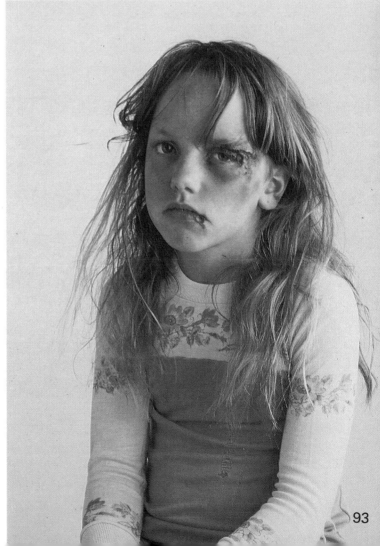

The effects of physical abuse may be visible, but they are often hidden by clothes. The damage is not only physical: the mind is battered as much as the body. The advice to any victim of physical abuse is to *seek help from a trusted adult* as soon as it is possible to do so safely. This may seem very obvious advice, but it is often not obvious to the victims of violence: many young people are so frightened and confused that they think there is nothing they can do except suffer in silence.

There are several help organisations, of which the largest is the National Society for the Prevention of Cruelty to Children, which deals with several thousand cases of abuse each year.

This NSPCC photograph is a realistic picture of a typical victim—although in this case we are in fact looking at a girl acting the part with the help of skilful make-up.

- *What does a sex abuser actually do?* There are several possibilities.

  He may spy on you (**Peeping Tom**) or he may expose his sex organs to you (**indecent exposure**). He may pester you on the telephone. He may try various tricks to get you to undress for him.

  More serious are the types of abuse in which he touches you.

  The affectionate touching and holding which we share with our parents, brothers and sisters, close relatives and friends, is a normal and important part of our relationships with them. It is a very different matter, however, when someone—whoever he may be—touches or holds you for his own sexual excitement, regardless of your feelings or rights.

  It may be difficult to draw the line between simple affection and sexual abuse—but stroking near or on the sex organs is *not* simple affection or normal behaviour.

  The abuser may go beyond stroking to masturbation. He may try to get you to masturbate him and, if you are a girl, he may even force you to have coitus with him. This is called **rape** and is a very serious crime (there is more about it on page 96).

  Some abusers try to force their penis into the mouth or anus of their victim, whether girl or boy: acts like these are called **indecent assault** and are just as serious as rape. Penetration of the anus is called **sodomy** (or **buggery**).

- *What should I do if someone abuses me?* Stop the abuser from going on—which may not be as difficult as you think.

  It may be very easy to go along with an abuser without realising what is happening. The moment when you do realise may be the worst possible moment to think clearly about what to do. So *now* is a good time to get your thoughts straight. The right reaction depends on whether you think your attacker is likely to be violent or not, and the alternatives are listed at the top of page 95 opposite. Please read this now.

  You will see that the advice is always *to seek help from a trusted adult.* Information and advice about how to do this is given in the panel headed 'Getting Help' on the facing page.

  Sexual abuse is very often disturbing and distressing. Even though *you* have done nothing wrong, you may still feel somehow guilty about the experience. What you have to do is to talk about it to somebody you trust as soon as you safely can.

  However embarrassed or scared you may be about telling anyone at all, however guilty or shocked you may feel, these feelings are likely to get worse the longer you keep things to yourself. Talking to somebody—sharing the burden—could be a great relief and the best way of bringing the abuse to an end.

  Even if you have been abused in the past and it has stopped, you should still seek help. By telling someone what has happened you may also be helping to prevent other young people being abused.

WHAT TO DO ABOUT A SEX ABUSER

if he is violent
or if you are worried that he may harm you:

- *do not resist*—you may just have to give in to him
- as soon as you safely can, seek help (see panel below)

if he is *not* violent
and if you think he is not likely to harm you:

- calmly, without inviting trouble, let him know that you will not do what he wants
- if necessary, and if you think you can do so safely, put up resistance
- as soon as you can, seek help (see panel below)

REMEMBER:

- many abusers can be stopped if you are firm
- if an adult is abusing you, normal ideas about being polite and obedient do not apply and should be ignored
- anyone who interferes with your body is violating your rights and committing a crime: he is the guilty one— *there is nothing for you to feel guilty about*

It is up to you to protect your rights. Don't be afraid to be firm with anyone who threatens them.

GETTING HELP

The vital thing is to find someone who can help, and that means talking about what has happened to you. If possible, talk to an adult you know and trust:

- the first choice is one of your parents or a close relative
- if no-one in the family is suitable, try your doctor, the school nurse, a teacher, your community policeman, or someone in your church or youth group.

Failing that, you can talk to someone you don't know; you have the choice of seeing, telephoning or writing to someone:

- *seeing or telephoning:* someone at one of the organisations listed on page 98
- *writing:* an 'agony aunt' on one of the national magazines or newspapers for information and advice or, for information only, NAYPCAS (address on page 98).

If you are unlucky in your first choice of adult to talk to (who may be unwilling to help or may not believe you) *do not give up*: keep trying until someone understands and does something to help.

You may prefer to contact one of the help organisations. *Do not worry* if you find it difficult to think or talk clearly about your problem. Their staff will be very sympathetic: they are used to helping people with problems and will not be embarrassed. You will not need to give your name or make a long statement: just answer their questions straightforwardly.

- *What can I do to protect myself against being abused?* It is a great pity that the trust and love which we all need should have to be guarded in any way but, as we have seen, some caution is necessary.

  There are several simple precautions which you can and should take as a matter of habit. The basic rules are listed in the panel below.

  You have no doubt been told not to talk to strangers. This is generally good advice, of course, but there *are* times when it is necessary to do so. That is why the rules given below avoid saying *never* talk to strangers.

  An abuser is always afraid of his victim talking about what he is doing and will try to press you into keeping quiet about it. *Don't keep quiet!* Never keep that sort of secret: find a trusted adult and talk about it.

- rape

  The force which a rapist uses on his victim may be physical or emotional (fear, threat or humiliation). In any event rape is a shocking experience. Apart from the shame, pain and terror which victims suffer at the time, it may have serious long-term consequences, both physical and mental. Many women become pregnant as a result of being raped.

  You may hear people say that a girl who is raped 'must have asked for it'. This is not only wrong and thoughtless: it is deeply hurtful and offensive to the victim. No man is *ever* justified in forcing a girl or woman to have sex with him: this is always an abuse and always rape.

- abuse in the family

  Unfortunately, many young people are abused by their father, step-father or other close relative. If you are in this unhappy situation, please make every possible effort to get help as quickly as you can. This may be the most difficult thing you have ever done, but you must somehow find the courage.

  If sexual abuse by a close relative includes coitus, it is called **incest**.

BEWARE STRANGERS!

OUTSIDE THE HOME AT ALL TIMES
all ages

- ALWAYS try to stick to regular routes, keep with other people and avoid isolated places whenever possible
- ALWAYS refuse to go in a car (or bus or train) with a stranger
- ALWAYS be extra careful in the dark

teenagers and children especially

- ALWAYS try to avoid talking to any stranger in places where help is not available if anything goes wrong
- ALWAYS be very suspicious indeed of strangers who claim to know you or who say they are bringing a message from someone you know
- NEVER accept any gifts from a stranger
- NEVER keep a secret if a stranger asks you to

AT HOME ON YOUR OWN

- NEVER let any stranger into the house *no matter how convincing or official or friendly* they seem to be—therefore it is safest if you:
- NEVER let any caller know that you are in the house at all
- NEVER let a telephone caller know that you are alone in the house
- ALWAYS keep the doors locked

- **substance abuse**

  Drugs are substances which affect the working of the body or mind in some way. They may be swallowed, inhaled or injected into the blood. The ones which people misuse (by taking them in unsafe quantities or when there is no need) are usually chosen for the moods and feelings which they create—generally because they are pleasurably relaxing or stimulating. They may also be addictive: that is, after taking them for a time people find it hard to stop taking them.

  The substances to beware are **illegal drugs**, **solvents**, **tobacco** and **alcohol**.

- **illegal drugs**: these are substances which it is illegal to possess, use or sell (unless, in some cases, they are prescribed by a doctor). They include **heroin** (also called junk, skag, smack, H), **cocaine** (coke, snow, charlie, the lady, a line), **cannabis** (marijuana or pot, grass, weed, hash) and **L S D** (lysergide or acid). They also include **amphetamines** (speed, uppers) and **barbiturates** (barbies, downers); and **tranquillisers**, although not illegal substances like the others, are abused in the same way.

  These drugs are all harmful or dangerous in one way or another, and you will be breaking the law if you use them. They are particularly dangerous if taken with alcohol, and the people who sell them often mix them with other substances which may themselves be harmful.

- **solvents**: many household products contain chemical solvents whose vapours make people who inhale them feel drunk. These include certain types of glue (used in **glue sniffing**) and various substances in aerosols. Aerosols are particularly dangerous, and so is the use of plastic bags to concentrate the vapour. A single 'sniff' can kill.

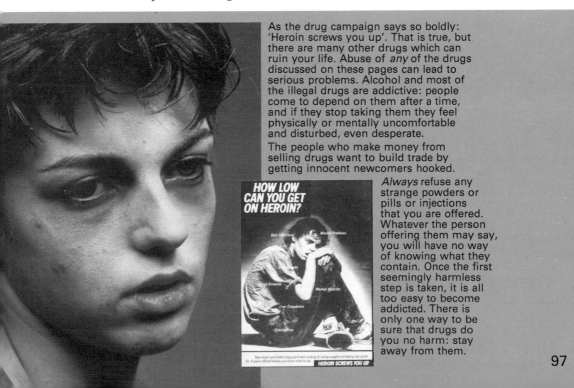

As the drug campaign says so boldly: 'Heroin screws you up'. That is true, but there are many other drugs which can ruin your life. Abuse of *any* of the drugs discussed on these pages can lead to serious problems. Alcohol and most of the illegal drugs are addictive: people come to depend on them after a time, and if they stop taking them they feel physically or mentally uncomfortable and disturbed, even desperate.

The people who make money from selling drugs want to build trade by getting innocent newcomers hooked.

HOW LOW CAN YOU GET ON HEROIN?

Always refuse any strange powders or pills or injections that you are offered. Whatever the person offering them may say, you will have no way of knowing what they contain. Once the first seemingly harmless step is taken, it is all too easy to become addicted. There is only one way to be sure that drugs do you no harm: stay away from them.

- **tobacco**: the nicotine and tar in tobacco cause many smokers to develop heart disease and certain kinds of cancer (chewing it is just as harmful). Heavy smokers foul the air for others, and non-smokers can get cancer from 'passive smoking'.

- **alcohol** is legal, socially acceptable, extremely popular and enjoyable. As a result its abuse does not stir up such strong feelings as does illegal drug abuse. Yet is is in a way the most dangerous of all these drugs. Drunkards injure or kill thousands of people on the roads each year, and there are about a million alcohol abusers in Britain.

- **temptation and addiction**

  Many young people as well as adults drink, smoke or take illegal drugs. They start out of boredom or to relax, to make themselves feel good or to try to escape from problems, to show off or because friends are doing it.

  The danger levels are very low. Even a few cigarettes a day or a pint or two of beer (much less for spirits, of course) will begin to damage your vital organs. The more you take the more quickly your brain or heart, lungs or other organs begin to suffer: it is as simple as that, and as inevitable. The quality of your life will suffer, and you may die at an earlier age. Whether you die in 2050 or 2040, for example, may seem too remote a choice to worry about today—but it *is* a choice, and the clock *is* ticking away.

  Many young people are already drinking or smoking by the time they leave school, and quite a few have started on illegal drugs. Most are well aware that these are harmful habits but, once started, few ever give them up.

  If you think you already have a problem with drugs or sniffing or alcohol, *get some help now.* If you cannot talk to your parents or to some other trusted adult, contact one of the organisations listed below.

  It may be very hard to resist the temptation to go along with what your friends do, and adults often set a bad example. Nevertheless, you do have a choice. You can only benefit by making the right choice.

ORGANISATIONS WHICH WILL HELP	**READ THIS FIRST**	Most of the following organisations have local offices or branches close to where you live. To find the branch nearest to you, look up the full name in your local telephone directory. Failing that, phone (or write to) the head offices given below

FOR HELP ABOUT PHYSICAL AND SEXUAL ABUSE	NATIONAL SOCIETY FOR THE PREVENTION OF CRUELTY TO CHILDREN (N S P C C)—*over 60 offices* Head office: 67 Saffron Hill, London EC1N 8RS (Phone: 01-242 1626) ROYAL SCOTTISH SOCIETY FOR THE PREVENTION OF CRUELTY TO CHILDREN (R S S P C C)—*over 20 offices* Head office: Melville House, 41 Polwarth Terrace, Edinburgh EH11 1NU (Phone: 031-337 8539) SAMARITANS: *a free and completely confidential emergency and befriending service—over 180 branches— phone (lines open 24 hours) or visit*
FOR HELP ABOUT SEXUAL ABUSE	RAPE CRISIS CENTRE: Phone: 01-837 1600—*line open 24 hours* INCEST CRISIS LINE: 32 Newbury Close, Northolt, Middlesex UB5 4JF (Phone: 01-422 5100—*line open 24 hours*)
FOR HELP ABOUT ALCOHOL OR DRUG ABUSE	ALCOHOLICS ANONYMOUS (A A): 11 Redcliffe Gardens, London SW10 9BQ (Phone: 01-352 9779) NARCOTICS ANONYMOUS (N A): Phone: 01-351 6794/6066—*help about any substance abuse problems* SAMARITANS: *see above*
INFORMATION ON LOCAL HELP ORGANISATIONS	CITIZENS ADVICE BUREAUX (C A B): *lots of information—phone or visit* NATIONAL ASSOCIATION OF YOUNG PEOPLE'S COUNSELLING AND ADVISORY SERVICES (N A Y P C A S)—*write on* 17-23 Albion Street, Leicester LE1 6GD STANDING CONFERENCE ON DRUG ABUSE (S C O D A)—*phone or write* 1-4 Hatton Place, London EC1N 8ND (Phone: 01-430 2341)

hygiene

Even before adolescence is reached, all children have become wholly responsible for their personal **hygiene** (which simply means the cleanliness of their bodies). As they approach adolescence, many young people become sensitive about the condition as well as the appearance of their bodies. Condition depends on diet, exercise and hygiene. Exercise generally is not a problem for young people, and diet is the subject of the next chapter. Here I want to give you some very important reminders about hygiene, particularly genital hygiene.

As we already know, everyone begins to sweat more during adolescence, particularly in the armpits, around the crotch and between the toes. This is quite natural, but if you do not wash these parts often the smell will be rather strong and unpleasant. Deodorants and anti-perspirants disguise body-smells, but they are not necessary: washing with soap and water is just as effective and much cheaper.

Girls must of course wash the vulva carefully. The tissue of the vulva and vagina is very delicate, and a girl must be very careful not to irritate it. No objects except tampons should be put inside the vagina; no deodorants or other sprays should be used; and it is also important to keep the fingernails short, smooth and very clean. Some girls are taught to shave off their pubic hair but this is quite unnecessary and serves no useful purpose.

During adolescence girls begin to have a discharge from the vagina: this is white and sticky and there may be more of it at some times than others. This is normal and there is no need to worry about it. However, if there is much more discharge than usual, or if it causes irritation or has a bad smell or changes colour, there may be an infection in the vagina. This is not likely to be serious, but it must be treated properly.

Menstrual blood can also sometimes have a slight smell, and you may find that your sweat smells stronger than usual during a period. The answer, of course, is to wash more often.

Boys must always wash the penis and scrotum very carefully. If you are not circumcised you must remember always to wash under the foreskin. It is normal to find a little sweat and a white soapy substance called **smegma** here, and unless these are washed away they will give off a bad smell and the smegma may cause you trouble.

Of course everyone knows that, to avoid the risk of any infection, careful hygiene after using the toilet is essential: the hands should *always* be washed carefully. Because the vulva is close to the anus, girls should always clean the anus by wiping from front to back, never from back to front.

If you are suffering from acne, check the last paragraphs on page 40.

diet

Adolescence is a time when the body grows very quickly: the extra flesh and bone we develop as we grow can come only from what we eat and drink. Most of us, particularly in adolescence, want both to be and to look healthy and attractive. For this reason, it is very important to think about what we eat and drink, and to know what is good and bad for us.

The food we eat is mainly made up of three things: **protein**, **fat** and **carbohydrate**. Most food contains a mixture of all three, but usually there is more of one than the others in each particular food.

Protein is found mostly in food from animals (for example lean meat, fish, chicken, milk and eggs) but also in things like nuts and beans. **Fat** is found mostly in butter, margarines, cooking oils and meat fat, and **carbohydrates** mostly in foods like flour, potatoes and rice (which all contain a lot of **starch**) and sugar.

Protein is important because as we grow up our muscles increase in size, and muscles are mainly made of protein. Young people who do not get enough protein may develop bodies which are weak and unhealthy.

Fat and carbohydrate have a different purpose: after they have been eaten, the body changes them into energy (that is, the power which enables us to move our limbs and keep our bodies warm). The energy value of any sort of food is measured in **kilocalories** or **kilojoules**, which you will often see on food labels. Carbohydrate and fat are just as necessary to the body as petrol is to a car. Someone who does not eat enough of them will feel weak and will become easily tired. On the other hand, someone who eats too much of them may have another problem: **overweight**.

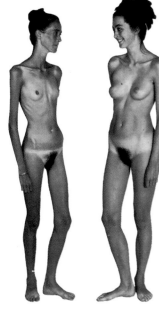

The taller of these two young women is very slim herself, but her sister has an eating problem as a result of which she is now *too* thin for her own good.

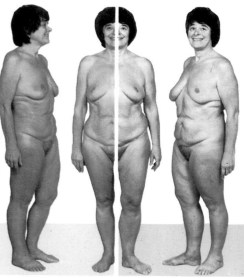

The woman on the right is overweight: the pictures on the left and right (taken three months apart) show the difference which nine kilos makes to her figure. Her natural weight is quite a few kilos less.

The amount of energy we need daily depends not only on our activities—walking, working, even breathing and sleeping—but also on our stature and age. Of course most people eat enough to meet their daily needs, but a few do not—perhaps because they do not bother or cannot afford to. Some very thin people (usually, but not only, adolescent girls) somehow manage to convince themselves that they are really fat and almost stop eating altogether; this is called **anorexia** and needs treatment by a doctor.

Much more common, however, is the opposite problem: very many people get into the habit of eating more food than they really need. This surplus food, instead of being turned into energy, is stored in the body as fat. If they become seriously overweight, we say they are suffering from **obesity**.

There are two other groups of substances which are essential for growth and health. These are **minerals** (for example iron, salt, calcium and iodine) and some special chemicals called **vitamins** (which are known by letters: A, B, C, D, and so on). The body needs only very small amounts of these substances, which are found in many foods (mostly in fresh vegetables and fruit, but also for example in fish, liver and milk). Eating too much of some of them, such as salt, can be harmful.

It is most important to have regular meals which contain some of all these things, and of course plenty of water as well. We call this a **balanced diet**. The study of diet is called **nutrition**, which also simply means feeding or nourishment; someone who is not eating enough, or not enough of the right things, is said to suffer from **malnutrition**.

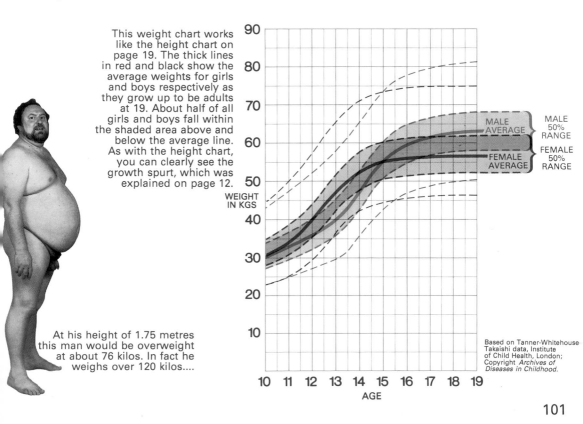

This weight chart works like the height chart on page 19. The thick lines in red and black show the average weights for girls and boys respectively as they grow up to be adults at 19. About half of all girls and boys fall within the shaded area above and below the average line. As with the height chart, you can clearly see the growth spurt, which was explained on page 12.

MALE AVERAGE
FEMALE AVERAGE
MALE 50% RANGE
FEMALE 50% RANGE

WEIGHT IN KGS

At his height of 1.75 metres this man would be overweight at about 76 kilos. In fact he weighs over 120 kilos....

Based on Tanner-Whitehouse Takaishi data, Institute of Child Health, London; Copyright *Archives of Diseases in Childhood*.

AGE

101

To sum up so far: the balanced diet we need for good health must include water, minerals and vitamins, and enough protein, fat and carbohydrate. Too little or—more often!—too much of any of these latter will lead to ill-health in one way or another. Often the eating habits of adolescents stay with them when they become adults, so that overfat young people are likely to grow into overfat, unhealthy adults.

In addition to fatness, certain types of fat and carbohydrate can cause, or make worse, various serious diseases. The most harmful fats, known as **saturated fats**, include not only the fat attached to meat but other animal-fat and dairy products like butter, cream and cheese. The fats known as **polyunsaturated fats**—such as fish oils and the vegetable oils made from seeds and nuts—are much less harmful.

The most harmful carbohydrates are sugars of every kind—white, brown, syrup, treacle, honey and so on—and cereals or flours which have been processed or refined. *Un*refined flours like wholemeal and pasta are much more healthy. Sugar in any form also has a very bad effect on your teeth. No matter how carefully you clean your teeth, some of the sugar will stick to them and they may begin to decay. Fluoride in the water helps to protect teeth, but not completely.

There is one other type of carbohydrate which is essential to our good health: **fibre** (also called **roughage**). Many people suffer from constipation (hard feces) and take laxatives to cure this: fibre is a natural material which prevents constipation and other bowel troubles. **High-fibre** foods (those with most fibre in them) are all plants: fruits, vegetables and grains.

Fruit and vegetables are also important in another way: if you do not eat enough of them your skin will begin to look unhealthy. (So-called 'skin foods' are useless, and a waste of money.)

Some people cannot eat particular foods because of **allergies**: that is, certain substances in these foods make their bodies break out in rashes. These substances may be natural or they may be artificial **additives**. Many processed foods contain additives, which are chemicals added to preserve them or to give them what the manufacturers think is a more attractive colour or flavour. More and more people prefer to avoid foods which have artificial ingredients and to keep to natural foods as far as possible.

In general, a healthier diet means eating *more* fresh, unprocessed high-fibre foods and *less* animal fats, sugar, salt and processed foods. If you do this, you will not need to worry about how much protein you are eating (it will be enough), or about counting calories.

With all this information to go on, we can now put together the healthiest type of diet. The main points appear in the panel below.

Here are some other useful guidelines for sensible eating:

- eat only when you are hungry— and stop before you feel full
- drink more water, especially before and during meals
- avoid processed foods (that is, convenience foods, packaged foods, 'junk food' and the like) because they generally contain a lot of hidden sugar, salt and saturated fat
- read the labels on packets, tins and bottles.

It is a worthwhile idea to develop healthy eating habits at the earliest possible age and then stick to them. Young people do not generally have much choice in the matter, because most meals are with the family or at school, but you should begin to try to control what you eat as soon as you have any say in the matter.

Perhaps you can make a start with a kitchen conference at home!

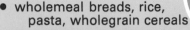

all you want

- wholemeal breads, rice, pasta, wholegrain cereals
- fresh fish, skinned chicken,
- skimmed milk, cottage cheese
- vegetables (fresh if possible)
- fruits (fresh, dried, unsweetened juices) and nuts

not too much

- red meat
- white bread, crisps
- eggs, full-cream milk, polyunsaturated margarines, yoghourt, cooking oils

very little

- fatty meats, sausages and other processed meats, meat pies
- butter, cream, hard cheese, lard, hard margarines
- sugar, sweets, chocolate
- sweet things like ice-cream, puddings, pastries, cakes, biscuits, jams, syrups
- fizzy drinks and squashes
- salt
- **all things fatty - sugary - salty**

Try to eat more from the range of foods in the green box as a change from those in the red box: they are just as tasty and much better for you.

t of these foods are in green 'all you want' box, two or three are in the er 'not too much' box and in the red 'very little' box. you see which these are?

life ahead

So far we have covered the physical facts of growth and reproduction. We have looked at the new physical and emotional experiences of adolescents, and at their new responsibilities related to self-care and sexuality.

Finally, we are going to look at the most important sexual issues and problems you are likely to meet in your relationships with other people. The main subjects are: your new sexual maturity, your sexual orientation, and your choice of adult life-style. There are three other matters which can be treated more briefly: the relationship between sex and love; sexually transmitted diseases; and conception and contraception.

- **sex and love**

Reproduction is by no means the only purpose of sex. Sex is also a way of expressing love and it is a source of pleasure.

Love, like sex, has several meanings. First, there are certain kinds of love which are not sexual: for example family love, between parents and children or between brothers and sisters, and the love of friends. Then there is the love between partners who make a deep commitment to one another. This is usually between a man and a woman in marriage, but it may exist just as deeply outside marriage, or between two people of the same sex; it is an emotional relationship and it probably also includes a sexual one.

Finally, 'making love' means having sex. Generally, however, sex is physical and love is emotional. There can be love without sex and sex without love.

Most religions recognise that sex is not only for reproduction but is also a proper expression of love, although they do not approve of the idea of sex simply for pleasure. Many young people, however, see sex much more in terms of love and pleasure than in terms of reproduction: like marriage, reproduction is for later in life.

Sex, in the sense of sexual activity, includes not only masturbation and coitus but also many other kinds of activity between partners which fall short of coitus (such as necking and petting). This is a big subject, and one for another book.

104

- **reaching sexual maturity**

After you reach sexual maturity (at the end of puberty) it takes a few more years to reach physical maturity (at the end of adolescence) and a few more still to reach emotional maturity (full adulthood). Those years represent the difference between being *able* to become a mother or father and being *ready* to become a parent.

In Britain today most young people reach sexual maturity at about 14 for girls and 15 for boys, and the average age of marriage is 23 for women and 25 for men. As you approach sexual maturity you may wonder what you are to do with your new abilities during those years.

Sexual maturity means several things. We have already looked at all of them separately, but it will be helpful now to bring them together. First, it means being fertile, having reached the age of menstruating or ejaculating. Secondly, it means having the physical ability to reach orgasm, to feel intense physical and sexual pleasure. Thirdly, it means experiencing the powerful instincts of the sex drive: the periodic need for sexual stimulation and satisfaction, and the urge to share these feelings with a partner.

Nature's purpose is reproduction, and in nature the physical events, the physical feelings and the emotions all go together. The urge to mate—to choose a partner and have coitus—leads naturally to conception and the birth of a baby.

The problem is that giving way to the natural urges—having sex because it feels good—leads to babies. We therefore have to control these sexual feelings, natural though they are—although it may not be easy to do so.

This can be a difficult problem for many young people. On the one hand they are in the grip of a powerful drive to express their sexuality in real life—and perhaps being urged on by friends to do so. On the other hand, their parents and other adults may be advising complete chastity—or, at best, advising them not to get involved in a sexual relationship for some years to come.

It is very hard for most teenagers to realise that the advice of the older generation may be worth listening to. Parents have very good reason to be concerned: they will almost certainly have been through the same sort of frustrations when they were adolescents. Young people often take huge risks without considering the consequences. The problems of unwanted babies and disabling diseases can be permanent ones.

All the stories and articles headlined here have appeared in national newspapers recently. Some papers favour sensational headlines, of course, but out of sight behind every incident the lives of many other ordinary people are affected, and there are countless other events going on every day which never get reported. Together with the sordid and shocking there is also, happily, much good news of achievement and goodwill— and quite a lot of humour.

105

- **sexual orientation**

  A very important part of our sexuality is the preference we have for sexual partners of a particular type: this is our sexual orientation.

  Most people are attracted to partners of the opposite sex (heterosexual), but many are naturally attracted to their own sex (homosexual) or to both sexes more or less equally (bisexual).

  At adolescence, most boys and girls develop a sexual interest in the other sex but, for reasons which are not well understood, some people's sexual feelings become fixed on others of their own sex. If this turns out to be the case with you, there is nothing to feel ashamed or guilty about: your preferences may be different from the majority, but there are millions of others like you.

  Homosexuals of both sexes are called gay; an alternative name for female homosexuals is lesbian. Most homosexuals do not look any different, or behave differently, from other people. Many marry and become mothers and fathers, and their orientation does not show in their everyday life.

  Most people find also that they are attracted to partners of about the same age as themselves, but many choose partners who are younger or older. The preferences may extend to other physical characteristics like height and shape, blue eyes, dark hair and so on. These are often powerful influences in the early stages of a relationship, but in due course the personality of the partner becomes more and more important.

  Sexual orientation towards a type of partner or activity which society regards as unnatural and harmful is called a deviation, and the person a deviant. We saw in the chapter on self-care that child abuse, rape and incest are deviations in this way.

- **life-styles**

  One of the most important decisions in your life will be your choice of life-style, for example whether to marry or not and whether to become a parent or not. Most of you will decide to get married and have children; most of the marriages will last (although in many cases one or both of the partners will have sex outside the marriage), but many will end in divorce.

  For this and other reasons there are hundreds of thousands of one-parent families in Britain today. Many of you will choose to live together and have children without getting married: about half-a-million couples live like this, and one baby in six is born outside marriage.

106

Many others of you will choose life-styles that do not involve marriage or children, and many more will break with convention and ignore the powerful unwritten rules of society by marrying or forming permanent partnerships across traditional boundaries like those of nationality or race, religion or sex.

- **discrimination**

Some of you will find as you grow up that you are discriminated against because of your sex, your skin colour, a physical disability, your sexual orientation or your chosen life-style.

The largest group discriminated against are women: a great many men (and some women) still hold the age-old view that women are inferior to men, the 'second sex'. Other minority groups which suffer discrimination include people of a different race from the majority, people of different races who marry, people who live together without marrying, the children of these last two groups, people who are disabled, and people who are homosexual or bisexual. These are all very large groups.

Discrimination usually operates very unfairly: most of the victims do not choose their status or possess any feature to justify their treatment—only that they were born different from the people around them.

- **STDs**

There are some diseases which affect the sex organs and are passed from one person to another only or usually during coitus or some other sexual activity. They are known as sexually transmitted diseases, usually called STDs (the old name was venereal diseases or VD).

STDs are the most common contagious diseases in the world. There are several different types, including gonorrhea and genital herpes and the most dangerous of them all: syphilis and Aids. Some are very harmful: they may infect an unborn child or cause sterility or some other permanent disability. One or two can kill.

STDs are spread through promiscuity: that is, having sex with more than one partner—catching a disease from one and and passing it on to others. Certain so-called 'safe sex' practices can reduce the risk but, apart from total abstinence, there is *only one way* to avoid the risk of catching an STD. This is fidelity with a single partner: that is, each partner has sex *only* with the other. This is a powerful argument for taking the greatest care when the time comes to choose a sexual partner.

Men | 107

- **conception and contraception**

Many married couples try for years to conceive a baby and fail; many adolescents have sex just once for fun—not wanting a baby at all and thinking 'it can't happen to me'—and the girl becomes pregnant. Failure to conceive and failure to avoid conception may be equally distressing.

Many couples have problems of infertility: the cause of this may be with the woman only, or the man only, or shared between them. Often medical help can be given to solve the problem, and new techniques are being developed all the time. Two of these new techniques, explained in the glossary, are artificial insemination and in vitro fertilisation.

Many fertile couples want to be able to continue to have sex without the risk of conception, in order to limit the size of their families and to ensure that their children are born at well-spaced intervals. This is called family planning (or birth control or planned parenthood), and various methods of avoiding conception—called contraception—have been developed.

There are three main types: contraceptives (special chemicals or devices which work in various different ways), so-called 'natural methods' (not using any contraceptive) and sterilisation (an operation which blocks the ovarian or sperm tubes permanently).

The most popular contraceptives are 'the Pill' for women and the condom for men, but there are several others which women can use. Some methods are very much more reliable than others, but *no* method of contraception is absolutely reliable. They all need to be used with the greatest care.

- **the 21st century**

The population of the world is expanding very rapidly indeed. Young people are maturing earlier and there is greater sexual freedom, both of which mean more pregnancies. Medical science and health services are developing rapidly, which means fewer miscarriages, still-births and infant deaths, and more adults are living longer.

There is an increasing trend towards smaller families, and family planning is becoming an important political issue in more and more countries. There is an even more important change taking place: in many countries of the world women are gaining an ever more powerful role in the family, in the community and in society.

All of you who are adolescents today are growing up into a society which will see more changes in your lifetime than there have been in the last hundred years. These will certainly include far-reaching developments in family planning, the treatment of STDs and sexual problems, as well as profound changes in attitudes to sex which will affect every family and each individual.

Your own children, born and growing up in the 21st century, may well be even more of a mystery to you than you are to your parents today.
Good luck!

Entering into a sexual relationship for
the first time carries adult responsibilities.
The decision to have sex is often taken
on the spur of the moment, but may be
regretted for a lifetime. By the time you
learn that a baby has been conceived,
it is too late to change your mind:
a new human life is already growing....

This picture of a 7-week-old embryo has become famous as
'the teardrop baby' in the 'pro life' versus 'pro choice' debate.

index

Principal text references and pictures are listed (but the foreword, introduction and glossary are not indexed).
Section and chapter titles, and other major references are in bold type, thus: diet **100-103**.
Pictures and captions are indicated by the letters 'p' and 'c' following the page number, thus: pubic bone 32pc.
Don't forget the glossary, pages 74-80.

other books

for young children

- THE BODY BOOK Claire Rayner/Piccolo 1979
  Excellent introduction to the subject; all colour
- HOW YOU BEGAN Lennart Nilssen/Kestrel 1975
  Reproduction and birth in fine photographs; colour, black and white
- NO MORE SECRETS FOR ME Oralee Wachter/Viking Kestrel 1985
  Realistic short stories alerting children to dangers of molesting
- WHERE DID I COME FROM? Peter Mayle/Macmillan 1978
  Imaginative introductory book, funny colour cartoons

for adolescents and adults

- ADOLESCENT SEX: Its Difficulties And Dangers ed. Ronald L. Kleinman/IPPF 1978
  Authoritative booklet especially helpful on STDs;
  from the International Planned Parenthood Federation, 18 Lower Regent Street, London SW1Y 4PW
- THE BODY Anthony Smith/George Allen & Unwin 1985
  Very substantial but exceptionally readable and fascinating study
- BOY, GIRL, MAN, WOMAN B.H.Claësson/Penguin 1980
  Frank information and advice for older teenagers (translated from Danish)
- A CHILD IS BORN Lennart Nilssen/Faber & Faber 1977
  Unique and brilliant photographic coverage; colour, black and white
- THE EIGHTIES EPIDEMIC: Drugs And Drug Abuse Freeman & Wood/Mirror Books—RSM 1986
  From Royal Society of Medicine, 1 Wimpole Street, London W1M 8AE; *in press*
- THE FACTS OF LIFE Susan Meredith & Robyn Gee/Usborne 1985
  Factual text; profusely illustrated with pop cartoons, all colour
- THE FACTS OF LOVE Alex & Jane Comfort/Mitchell Beazley 1979
  Perceptive, sensitive survey for teenagers; illustrated
- FOETUS INTO MAN Professor J. M. Tanner/Open Books 1978
  Masterly study of human growth for lay readers
- GROWING PAINS Claire Rayner/Heinemann Quixote Press
  Invaluable and wide-ranging practical help for teenagers
- HAVE YOU STARTED YET? Ruth Thomson/Piccolo 1980
  Clear down-to-earth advice on menstruation
- THE OSTRICH POSITION Carol Lee/George Allen & Unwin 1986
  Illuminating and thought-provoking inside view of sex education
- OU GUIDE TO HEALTHY EATING Rambletree Pelham 1985
  Informative survey from Open University and Health Education Council
  (also BBC booklet based on this: YOU ARE WHAT YOU EAT)
- PREGNANCY BOOK Health Education Council 1984
  Excellent (and free) guide, fully illustrated in colour
- PREVENTING CHILD SEXUAL ASSAULT Michele Elliott/Bedford Square Press 1985
- THE WILLOW STREET KIDS: It's Your Right To Be Safe Michele Elliott/Andre Deutsche 1986
  Essential reading for all parents by founder of Kidscape, 82 Brook Street, London W1Y 1YG
- THE WHICH? GUIDE TO BIRTH CONTROL Penny Kane/Consumer Association 1983
  Thorough survey of contraception methods and services

Valuable reading lists are available from:
- Family Planning Association Book Centre, 27-35 Mortimer Street, London W1N 7RJ
- Health Education Council, 78 New Oxford Street, London WC1A 1AH

Apart from the FPA and HEC, the following organisations publish useful booklets and leaflets:
- British Medical Association, BMA House, Tavistock Square, London WC1H 9JP
- National Marriage Guidance Council, Little Church Street, Rugby, England
- National Society for the Prevention of Cruelty to Children, 67 Saffron Hill, London EC1N 8RS

A substantial review by Janet Newman, SEX EDUCATION: A CRITICAL EVALUATION OF MATERIALS, with an excellent introduction, was published in 1979 by the LA Youth Library, Paradise, Birmingham B33HQ; now out of print.

At your local library you may find useful books located, for example, under the following headings:
adolescence (shelves 136, 155, 301); biology (574); human growth (573); physiology (612); psychology (132).